# Ecumenism
# in
# Transition

# Ecumenism in Transition

A Paradigm Shift

in the Ecumenical Movement?

Konrad Raiser

WCC Publications, Geneva

*Translated from the German by Tony Coates*

Cover design: Rob Lucas

ISBN 2-8254-0996-0

© 1991 English edition, WCC Publications, World Council of Churches, 150 route de Ferney, 1211 Geneva 2, Switzerland

Printed in Switzerland

Original title: Ökumene im Übergang

© 1989 Chr. Kaiser Verlag, München

# Contents

# Instead of a Preface

Witten, March 1988

Dear Philip,

Since my return from Geneva to the Federal Republic almost five years ago, I have been repeatedly asked whether I would commit to writing something of my experiences during my fourteen years of work with the World Council of Churches. My move to the totally new profession of a university professor and the manifold demands made by ecumenical work here have kept me so busy that I have only had time to prepare lectures and write occasional articles. Thus, references to my personal evaluation of the results of my years in Geneva are to be found tucked away in quite a few places in my occasional publications of recent years, as, for example, in my short contribution to the book produced as a tribute to you by Pauline Webb. Other references have found their way into my lectures and have been heard only by my students in Bochum. But we teachers have an undeserved privilege of applying for a sabbatical after four years' teaching and I have used it to write down in a connected way some of my thoughts from recent years, looking back on my time in Geneva and considering the future of the ecumenical movement.

When you read this book, you will perhaps say: "Now he has definitely become a German academic theologian!" I learned during my years in Geneva to accept the undeniable marks of my German ecclesiastical, theological and social context. You encouraged me and all your collea- gues to accept our context, because you were, and are, convinced that only in that way is genuine dialogue possible.

But I also hope that, as you read my thoughts, you will detect how much I have learned from my conversations with you and other ecumeni- cal companions on the way. Much of this is only too difficult to communicate in my present context. You know that from your own comparable experience in Jamaica. And you know better than I the tension between commitment and rootlessness, which is the experience of all of us who have got fully caught up in the ecumenical movement. I can deal with that tension better in the somewhat distanced language of academic theology.

Shortly after the Vancouver assembly in 1983, it became clear to me that I wanted to attempt to take up and develop that vision of the "ecumenical house" which you portrayed in your magnificent report, and which found no response in Vancouver. Our symposium at Cartigny in October 1984 shortly before your departure strengthened that desire. Whether the attempt I have made here — and it is no more than an attempt — proves to be a worthy contribution, I must leave it to others to judge. I was, however, surprised at what I found when I set about testing and developing my initial intuition. I discovered connections that had not occurred to me before, and finally, to my amazement, that despite all the widening of ecumenical horizons I had remained faithful to myself and to the theses at the end of my dissertation of almost twenty years ago.

It seems to me that we have arrived at a decisive moment of transition for the future of the ecumenical movement. Other friends — perhaps including you yourself — may draw the lines in another direction. But, above all, it seems important to me that the conversation should be started up again and that all partners in ecumenical dialogue should give up the defensive attitude which has characterized so many debates in recent years. Despite its academic appearance, this book is intended to be no more than one contribution among others to this essential discussion. I am not concerned to reach established conclusions, but to engage in critical dialogue with those who, like myself, see the ecumenical movement as their vocation.

I would thus wish to dedicate this book to you as the senior member of the "ecumenical household" and a trusty companion on the way, in the hope that it will stimulate you and other friends to consider "ecumenism in transition" together — perhaps at a second Cartigny symposium. If, as Ernst Lange said in the last letter in his book *And Yet It Moves:* "Ecumenism can no longer be toyed with as a mere possibility. It has become the test case of faith", then such reflection is not merely a luxury to be indulged in by a German professor on a sabbatical, but an essential task for us all. I know that you and I are agreed on this, and therefore this book shall be yours first of all.

Yours in cordial friendship,

Konrad

# 1. *Uncertainty in the Ecumenical Movement*

## 1. The present situation

Whenever in recent times an attempt has been made at a diagnosis of the ecumenical movement, the overwhelming impression has been one of stagnation if not resignation. To demonstrate this, one has only to point to the fate of the three major ecumenical initiatives of recent years which have excited widest public interest: the Lima text on *Baptism, Eucharist and Ministry*; the report and recommendations of the Joint Ecumenical Commission on the examination of the sixteenth-century condemnations; and the "conciliar process" for Justice, Peace and the Integrity of Creation. All three initiatives were at first enthusiastically welcomed: quite a few people felt that with them the decisive breakthrough was coming within reach — but, after a short while, all the old reservations had reasserted themselves. Certainly, any such diagnosis is a matter of perspective, and the belief "And yet it moves!" boldly held by a number of ecumenical companions is not implausible. But the case for it rests on such nice distinctions that it is barely able to affect public opinion or even the general ecumenical climate. Has the momentum run out? Have all the ecumenical trump cards been played?

If a comparision is made between the present situation and the ecumenical breakthrough of the late 1960s, the difference becomes strikingly clear. Now, this observation holds equally good for almost all other areas of public life — political, social and cultural. The ecumenical movement has always been extraordinarily sensitive to such changes in public awareness, and so its present stagnation may also be seen as reflecting a general loss of direction. But have there not also been times when the ecumenical movement has gone against the spirit of the age? Does it not have its own source of strength and standards of integrity? The interaction we observe between public awareness and the ecumenical movement should not in any case be seen as being determined in one direction only. That would provide no answer to the question as to how future progress can be made. Do we have to be content with glorifying the late 1960s as the "golden age" of maximum ecumenical openness and limiting ourselves today to protecting, defending or — worst of all — administering past achievements?

A serious diagnosis of the present situation of the ecumenical movement must in any case attempt to reach a clearer understanding of the nature and causes of the changes which have taken place in the last twenty years. Such attempts have repeatedly been made, and they can be of help in clarifying the conditions with which any future-oriented approach will have to come to terms. A series of these factors will be identified later. Their effects are related to the fact that until the end of the 1960s the ecumenical movement had a constantly expanding profile. The WCC Uppsala assembly of 1968 has become symbolic of this perception of ecumenical concerns as being all-inclusive. This applies both to the interconfessional and the intercultural dimension of the ecumenical movement.

Since then ecumenical work has now become inconceivable without the active participation of the Roman Catholic Church and all the churches of the Orthodox tradition. As we look back, the effects of this new inclusiveness become increasingly clear. At the same time a development has taken place that has made the ecumenical fellowship of churches a worldwide fellowship in the fullest sense, symbolized by the entry into the WCC of a great number of churches in countries in the southern hemisphere. The search for independence in the major ecumenical regions has meanwhile also become a decisive factor. The international dimension of the ecumenical movement has been linked since Uppsala with the key words: racism, development and liberation, human rights, interfaith dialogue, etc. The orientation of ecumenical work towards the problems of justice and peace in the human community in our shrinking world runs like a scarlet thread through the developments of the last twenty years. Of course, not all the features in the overall ecumenical profile at the time of the Uppsala assembly which I have mentioned were completely new. But there was then a qualitative leap forward towards a real universality in the ecumenical movement.

It is possible to see the difficult internal debates of these last twenty years as the consequent effects of this qualitative leap forward. What was at first welcomed and hailed as the fruit of long years of effort proved more and more to be a tense holding together of elements which refused to be reconciled, either theoretically or practically. Thus three differing profiles of the ecumenical movement have emerged more and more starkly. They are all indeed related under the one roof of the WCC, but in actual performance they rapidly reach the point where communication breaks down. At the risk of gross simplification, I would characterize these three profiles of ecumenism as: ecclesiastical, cultural-social, and intellectual-pedagogical. One can also speak of the "interconfessional", the "intercultural" and the "intersubjective" forms of ecumenism.

However these forms of ecumenism are described and characterized, there can, I think, be no doubt that the new level of perception of the universal range of ecumenism achieved at Uppsala has resulted in the divergence of these different forms of ecumenism. This development raises the question of the internal integrity and coherence of the ecumenical movement. Is there, in fact, such a thing as the "one ecumenical movement" which was expressly evoked at the beginning of the cooperation between the Roman Catholic Church and the World Council of Churches? Is the present stagnation perhaps a consequence of the unresolved conflict between the various forms of ecumenism, all of which declare their allegiance to the "unity" of the ecumenical movement, but do not all understand the same thing by it?

As early as 1972, Ernst Lange, reflecting on the newly formulated functions and tasks of the WCC, was speaking of the threefold uncertainty of the ecumenical movement: uncertainty as regards goals, methods and the level of real support. His observations are worth examining again in today's changed circumstances.[1]

## 2. Uncertainty as regards goals

What is the goal of the ecumenical movement? In any attempt to produce a concise definition of its goal the key-word "unity" inevitably appears. Again and again the raison d'etre of the ecumenical movement is linked with this goal. But there have always been in addition other goals in which the various origins of the ecumenical movement find expression: mission, responsibility for the world, renewal. The revised WCC constitution, on which Ernst Lange based his observations, places together the various goals in article 3: it begins with unity, and then goes on to mention common witness and mission, service and renewal. This explicit statement of goals was at that time a distinct advance on the formal statements of the earlier version of the constitution. But the juxtaposition of the various functions and goals conceals the unresolved tensions. Is church unity, the promotion of human community in justice and peace, or the spiritual, missionary and ecumenical renewal of the churches the foremost goal of the ecumenical movement? It must, moreover, constantly be emphasized that the ecumenical movement and the WCC are not identical; thus, for example, the Roman Catholic Church, which is not a member church of the WCC, formulates in its Decree on Ecumenism its own conception of the bases and goals of the ecumenical movement. And other interchurch organizations exist to serve the churches in their confessional or practical work together.

## 2.1. Unity

Is the "goal of visible unity in one faith and in one eucharistic fellowship expressed in worship and in common life in Christ"[2] unambiguous? In the years since this formulation of the article in the WCC constitution was adopted after difficult debate to reach understanding, wide and intensive discussion has taken place on the goal of unity and the path to it. Despite all the clarity meanwhile achieved on the steps towards unity, there appears at this precise point a deep-lying uncertainty. It stems from an unresolved tension in the formulation of the goal. Are we speaking here of the "unity of the church" or of the "unity of the churches"? Is the goal to make "visible", to manifest the unity of the church given in Christ, or is it a matter of restoring broken unity, of overcoming the schism or schisms that have arisen in the course of church history? Or, to put it another way: is the reference point for the achievement of the goal of unity a theological understanding of unity with a Christological, Trinitarian or eschatological foundation, that approaches critically all existing achievements; or does the quest begin with the existing situation of separated churches, which are to be got moving towards more visible unity? The discussion on models of unity, which took place particularly in the 1970s, is an expression of this unresolved tension. It seems to me, moreover, that these issues have not been properly clarified to this day.

Within the WCC a basic consensus developed in the years up to 1961 which found expression in the well-known statement on unity by the third assembly at New Delhi. The unity of the church is given in Jesus Christ once for all. It is rooted in the Trinitarian unity of the Father with the Son in the Holy Spirit. As the determinative foundation of the church it has not been lost, but it has been obscured by the divisions of church history. Unity is thus "God's gift and our task". The church is called ever anew to make visible its essential unity and to manifest it in fellowship, witness and service. Unity is thus not primarily an interchurch issue. In the question of unity in each church and at all levels of church life, it is rather basically a matter of the church being the church. While in the period after the New Delhi assembly particular stress was placed on the unity of "all in each place" in "fully committed fellowship", since Uppsala consideration has been principally directed to the unity of churches which are separated from one another in space and time. The statements of the Nairobi assembly on unity in "conciliar fellowship" mark the provisional conclusion of these efforts to clarify the goal of unity.

The determinative presupposition behind this goal is the effectiveness of the so-called Christological method, i.e. the belief that a common reference back to Jesus Christ and the convergence of all churches to him will so relativize and "soften" their differences and opposing viewpoints in doctrine, order and life that they will move to a position where they can make their fellowship ever more comprehensively visible. If historic differences are viewed and interpreted from this reference point, the value placed on them changes. This is the intrinsic assumption of the so-called Lima text on *Baptism, Eucharist and Ministry*, which, it must be admitted, has hardly been brought out in the debate.

This understanding of unity, however, has from the beginning not passed unchallenged. As early as 1961, the Orthodox delegates to the New Delhi assembly felt compelled to register a minority vote against it. They regarded the statement on unity as an expression of a Protestant approach to ecumenical debate aiming at overcoming the juxtaposition and opposition of denominations and confessions, which are in principle equal.

> For the Orthodox the basic ecumenical problem is that of schism... The unity has been broken and must be recovered. The Orthodox church is not a confession, one of many, one among the many. For the Orthodox, the Orthodox church is just the church. [3]

In fact, the dual expression "God's gift and our task" does correspond to a basic Protestant principle, which is alien to Orthodox tradition. For Orthodox, the one church of the creed is given visibly in the Orthodox church, which has stood, and still stands, in unbroken continuity with the undivided church of the early centuries. The Orthodox church thus exists among the other Christian churches as the faithful witness to the true unity of the church. As to how schism can be healed, there are various opinions even within Orthodoxy. But in any case, scepticism towards the attempt to seek agreements and consensus by way of interchurch doctrinal conversations is deep-rooted, even though the Orthodox have recently entered into official conversations with the Roman Catholic and Lutheran churches, while similar conversations have already been conducted over a longer period with Old Catholics and Anglicans.

This dissent from the Protestant ecumenical approach has meanwhile also been clearly voiced in the field of Roman Catholicism. It is expressed in publicly stated hesitations towards "ecumenism of negotiation",[4] which may indeed produce significant growing together in the human sphere, but not unity itself. More clearly now than at the time immediately after the Second Vatican Council, the concept of "entering into unity with Rome" stands in the foreground rather than the restoration of unity. It was, in fact, the Roman Catholic Church which, after the Council, entered into a multiplicity of bilateral doctrinal conversations with other churches, and thus gave rise to the model of "ecumenism of negotiation". But there has never been any doubting of the belief that the one church of the creed is embodied in the Roman Catholic Church. Since the universal dogmatic and legal structure belongs inalienably to this model of unity, which finds visible form in communion with the pope, here too what we are ultimately dealing with is simply how to overcome the break in the unity of the church, which has come about by bodies splitting off from the one church. Like the Orthodox church, the Roman Catholic Church claims to stand in unbroken continuity with the church of the early centuries. While it is true that the pre-Vatican II demand that the separated churches should "return" is no longer current, all other ways come up against this unambiguous barrier in the self-understanding of the Roman Catholic Church. There is this enduring hope that hearts and minds will be converted by the Spirit of God.

It would be avoiding the core of the problem if we saw here an indication of an ecumenical change of course on the part of the Roman Catholic Church. The unresolved tension is even included in the documents of the Second Vatican Council itself, as O.H. Pesch has recently demonstrated in a penetrating study of the Decree on Ecumenism.[5] He points to the clear signs of a "relativizing" of the exclusive dogmatic self-understanding; that does not lessen the inconsistency, but virtually makes it logically insoluble. In any case, according to Pesch, it would be to deceive ourselves to hope that the Roman Catholic Church could adopt the basic model of the WCC,

> according to which the unity of the church has been lost, and now the churches as it were sit in a circle around their centre, Christ, in order to seek again first of all the unity intended by their Lord.[6]

Although this representation of the basic model of the WCC can, in the light of what has been said above, certainly be critically questioned, it does give a clear picture of the problem.

The uncertainty in the ecumenical movement regarding the goal of unity comes out in many individual problems, which I cannot deal with in detail here. As I see it, in all instances there stands in the background the tension between a conception of ecumenism which has as its goal "making visible" or "manifesting" the unity which is given, and another conception, which consists in "restoring" or "incorporating into" an existing unity. Leaving that tension aside, there is, of course, a wide area of agreement on the foundation and development of the goal of unity. It is thus not disputed that unity belongs to the essence of the church, to its *esse* and not merely to its *bene esse*. Unity is rooted in the Trinitarian communion of the Godhead; through the work of the Holy Spirit the church shares in this divine unity. All who confess Jesus Christ and are baptized in his name are incorporated into the body of Christ by the Holy Spirit. Between them there is a basic relationship, which does not have to be first created. The ecumenical movement is itself a work of the Holy Spirit and its goal is the visible unity of all Christians and churches. There is, finally, widespread agreement that the visible unity of the church must at least satisfy the following criteria: a common confession of faith, a common understanding and common practice of the sacraments, especially baptism and the eucharist, mutual recognition of ministries, and a structure enabling the parts of the one church to make common decisions, when circumstances make it necessary.

In the end, however, agreement on the goal of unity presupposes clarification of the outstanding ecclesiological questions. If, in the unity issue, it is a matter of what it means to be the church, of the nature of the church itself, then it is not surprising that the uncertainty over the goal and the way to it can be traced back to a basic ecclesiological difference. In other words: it is a matter of determining the relationship between Christ and his church.

*2.2. Human community in justice and peace*

It has always been a commonly accepted belief that the unity of the church as the goal of the ecumenical movement is not a goal for its own sake. Unity must result in witness and service in the world. The gathering together and sending out of the church belong indissolubly together. The extract from the WCC constitution quoted above continues after describing the goal of unity, "... and to advance towards that unity in order that the world may believe". In particular, the relation between unity and mission as ecumenical goals and as basic dimensions in the understanding of ecumenism was the object of lively debate in the early years of the WCC.[7]

The previously mentioned qualitative leap forward at the Uppsala assembly towards a real universality strengthened the conviction that ecumenism must be understood in the light of its Greek root "oikoumene", i.e. as concerning "the whole inhabited earth". The goal of the ecumenical movement could thus not be the unity of the church in its narrow sense but must be the unity of humankind in justice and peace. The biblical vision of God's shalom, which had been rediscovered in the course of ecumenical discussion on mission, was taken up and used as a basis for this wider understanding of unity. Other attempts to find a basis began from the Christological confession of the incarnate Son of God as the founder of a new humanity, which embraced all human beings, all peoples, in its intention, or from the theme of Christ's kingly rule over the church and the world, which has as its goal the establishment of his kingdom in peace and justice. Seen in this perspective, the church and humankind are not essentially different. The church is rather that part of humankind which confesses and testifies to the new humanity in Christ, the divine shalom. Indeed, the church's raison d'etre, its missionary task, consists in witnessing and working for the new human community in justice and peace, participating in God's action in history, in which he realizes his shalom, and so symbolically anticipating that new reality. Seen in this light, the church could be described as "the agent of a coming world community".

This extension and shift of the goal of the ecumenical movement had received emphatic support from the documents of the Second Vatican Council and their consequent repercussions. Thus the Dogmatic Constitution on the Church stated that:

> the church, in Christ, is in the nature of sacrament — a sign and instrument, that is, of communion with God and of unity among all men.[8]

It seemed as if the Uppsala assembly a few years later was echoing that Council document when it said:

> The church is bold in speaking of itself as the sign of the coming unity of mankind.[9]

The orientation towards the whole of humanity received emphatic support from the Pastoral Constitution *Gaudium et Spes* and from the encyclical

*Populorum Progressio*, with its statement: "Development is the new name for peace."[10]

Against this background there developed in subsequent years a wide spectrum of new ecumenical activities and, at least initially, there was a positive expectation that, leaving aside all ecclesiological difficulties, it would be possible to build up close cooperation between the WCC member churches and the Roman Catholic Church. The joint Committee on Society, Development and Peace (SODEPAX), set up for this purpose, ran admittedly into difficulties after the expiry of its first mandate in 1971, and in 1980 this organizational form of cooperation, which had begun with such high hopes, was brought to an end.[11]

However, there were also problems within the WCC with this new approach. The fundamental theological study programme of the Commission on Faith and Order "The Unity of the Church and the Unity of Humankind" visibly retreated from the universal human perspective and concentrated on reflection, in itself important and creative, on fundamental ecclesiological issues in the light of the conflicts tearing the human community apart. All attempts to find a theological foundation for ecumenical commitment to justice and development, to liberation and human rights, against racism and sexism, as an indispensable expression of the ecumenical calling, ran increasingly up against the polarized argument between "ecclesiastical ecumenism" and "secular ecumenism".

The debate on these issues, which has been conducted at times with great passion, cannot and should not be repeated here. The uncertainty of the ecumenical movement regarding its goals can be brought out clearly in this series of questions: Is work for justice and peace an expression of Christian responsibility in the social and political realm, or is it central to the church's confession of faith? How far can and may the ecumenical movement go in solidarity and support for social and political initiatives and movements outside the bounds of the church? How do the priestly task to reconcile and the prophetic task to expose sin and fight against injustice relate to each other?

The area in which these questions have been thought through most intensively is the ecumenical involvement in the struggle against racism. The Programme to Combat Racism has been constantly criticized as a symbol of the alleged falling away of the WCC from the central goals of the ecumenical movement, i.e. to work for the unity of the church. Against this criticism, it has become more and more clear that in the struggle against racism we are not dealing with a "normal" political problem but with a challenge to the integrity of the church. Racism is sin, a blatant violation of God's will. The theological justification of racist structures must be condemned as heresy. This is not a matter of "heresy" in a figurative, ethical, sense. Heresies are a challenge to the essential being of the church, not simply to the truth of a particular belief. Racism is a heresy in that basic sense of the word: under the appearance of credal legitimacy it undermines the unity of the church. The church must therefore oppose racism with a concrete confession of its unity founded on Christ, a confession which includes a denial of the forces of division. Talk of reconciliation is only appropriate in a context of actual change and repentance, where existing injustice is removed and put right.

These insights have affected other areas of social involvement, such as, for example, issues of the spirit, logic and practice of deterrence and the conflict between rich and poor. Here, too, it is not simply a matter of what are certainly urgent questions of ecumenical responsibility for the world but also of challenges to the integrity of the church as a symbolic community, in which the new humanity in Christ is taking shape. But the uncertainty of the ecumenical movement has become apparent once again in the invitation to a conciliar process with as its goal a covenant for Justice, Peace and the Integrity of Creation. Earlier, the Lutheran World Federation had had the same experience with its declaration of a *status confessionis* regarding apartheid in South Africa. The uncertainty arises from the double tension between the church's work of reconciliation or prophetic witness on the one hand, and on the other between the ecumenical goals of the unity of the church or justice and peace in human society.

The Vancouver assembly took clear note of this tension (as have other previous documents, e.g. the letter to member churches, Utrecht, 1972),[12] in the report of the issue group on "Taking Steps Towards Unity":

> At this assembly we have sensed a tension between some of those who are concerned with the unity of the church and others concerned with the desperate need for justice, peace and reconciliation in the human community. For some, the search for a unity in one faith and one eucharistic fellowship seems, at best secondary, at worst irrelevant to the struggles for peace, justice and human dignity; for others the church's political involvement against the evils of history seems, at best secondary, at worst detrimental to its role as eucharistic community and witness to the gospel.
>
> As Christians we want to affirm there can be no such division between unity and human renewal, either in the church or in the agenda of the WCC.[13]

The Assembly thus recommended that earlier studies on the unity of the church in its relation to the unity of humankind be resumed under the new title "The Unity of the Church and the Renewal of Human Community". It must be admitted that the existing documentation from this study process, which concentrates on the issue of the church as mystery and prophetic sign, in particular in the context of the problem of the community of women and men in the church and the struggle for justice, confirms the existence of this tension rather than overcoming it. [14]

## 2.3. Renewal and spirituality

One final conflict of goals can be briefly mentioned. It arises out of the understanding and practice of ecumenical renewal. From the beginning the ecumenical movement had as a goal renewal in the life of the churches and their members, for it was evident that the churches in their inherited form and practice were not able to rise to the newly perceived call to unity and mission, witness and service. The early ecumenical movement thus explicitly understood itself to be a renewal movement. In its efforts for renewal from the Bible and for active witness by lay people, it took up again central themes from the Reformation. The ecumenically inspired attempts at church reform in the 1960s were echoed in the reform of the Roman Catholic Church in the course of the Second Vatican Council and were reinforced by it. Once again the Uppsala assembly, with its theme "Behold, I Make All Things New", represents a high point in these efforts for ecumenical renewal. It took place in an atmosphere of widespread radical change in society. The two sections on "Worship" and "Towards New Styles of Living" clearly revealed the desire for renewal. They also pointed to the need for changed structures in church and society and for a new Christian life-style. The recurring theme in this concern was participation by Christians in change.

What has become of this impulse towards the ecumenical renewal of the churches in the intervening twenty years? By means of highlighting two developments, the shift of emphasis during that period can be clearly shown. The first development: the debate on *ministry*. When the Commission on Faith and Order took up again the issue of ministry in 1964, the discussion was clearly centred on a fresh understanding of the unity of ministries in the church. [15] The insight that all lay people as members of the people of God had received through baptism a ministry in the church and the experience of missionary work made it necessary to review the traditional theological foundation and the form of the ordained ministry. From 1972, under Orthodox and Roman Catholic influence, the emphasis changed and the issue of the ordained ministry became once again the central concern. Since then the result of these efforts has appeared in the section on ministry in the ecumenical convergence document, or "Lima text": in it the interest in renewal of all ministries in the church is pushed into the background and replaced by an attempt to make the classical, threefold pattern of the ordained ministry ecumenically binding.[16] Renewal by a return to tradition, perhaps?

The second development is the debate on *worship* and *liturgy*. The work by the Uppsala assembly on the theme of worship revealed the tension between the attempt on the one hand to take secularized society totally seriously and on the other to recover an understanding of liturgy which, while being celebrated *in* the world, was not *of* the world. The tension was also not resolved in a subsequent study of the Commission on Faith and Order.[17] But here also the emphasis has shifted more and more clearly in a high-church liturgical direction. It is thus not surprising that the Lima liturgy stands today as a symbol of the ecumenical renewal of worship. So is this too renewal through revival of ancient tradition?

These two developments show clearly the tension between continuity and change as the basic problem in all efforts at ecumenical renewal. Does renewal have as its goal a new form of church, which can do justice to God's commission in a changed world, or does renewal mean rather recovering continuity with the origins of the church and its witness? That question, which has as yet received no real answer, is the key to understanding the uncertainty of the ecumenical movement as regards the call to renewal.

An important clue to understanding this development lies in the phrase "crisis of spirituality", which had already appeared in the early 1970s. The earlier positively accepted movement for change gave way to an analysis in which attention centred on identifying the symptoms of the crisis. Are we here dealing with a "crisis of faith" in the secularized world, or is it rather a "crisis of obedience" for believers in face of worldwide injustice? Is it a matter of "spiritual renewal" or rather of a "renewal of Christian practice"? In the lively ecumenical debate on these questions, it seemed at first that, with the help of formulas such as "struggle and contemplation" (Taizé) or "spirituality for combat" (David Jenkins/M.M. Thomas), these two poles of tension could be successfully bound together, thus holding together "being" and "doing" in reciprocal relationship.[18]

In later developments, however, this tension, influenced by crises which became more and more acute, developed into increasingly sharp opposition. On the one hand, the biblical tradition of spiritual warfare was rediscovered. The Christian life in the eschatological expectation of the kingdom of God is a constant warfare, in which the power of the new life springing from the resurrection wrestles with the powers of death.

> Our struggle is not against flesh and blood. It is against the principalities, against the powers of evil... [19]

It is a struggle for the confession of the one God against the manifold false gods of power, property and security. This dimension of a "spiritual struggle" was a feature of many of the statements to come out of the Vancouver assembly. [20]

On the other hand, "spirituality" became the keyword of the efforts for "spiritual renewal" and for "spiritual ecumenism" in critical distinction to the various forms of "social ecumenism". Spiritual ecumenism, in the sense of "change of heart and holiness of life" had already been described in the Decree on Ecumenism of the Second Vatican Council as "the soul of the whole ecumenical movement". [21] In fact, the hope for spiritual renewal and conversion offered the only solution to the logical contradiction as regards achieving the unity of the church. Consequently, the original impetus for renewal was increasingly taken back into the sphere of the inner life: prayer for unity, questions of individual life-style, the quest for ecumenical spirituality practised in community took the place of efforts to change the structures. So the churches are alert to signs of spiritual, charismatic renewal, but react allergically to demands for structural change.

What is the goal of the ecumenical movement? Is it a church renewed in its social form and work, which is able to serve the renewal of human community, or is it a renewal and deepening of Christianity's traditions of belief and piety, which complement one another in "reconciled diversity"? Can the church expect decisive ecumenical renewal only from God's new-creating action through the Spirit, or is renewal at the same time a question of changing one's ways, of active obedience to the call of God, which is not for the church alone but for the whole of humanity?

## 3. Uncertainty as regards methods

Uncertainty as regards the goals of the ecumenical movement affects the methods used to pursue those goals. Here too it is not simply a matter of competing methods used by the three different profiles of the ecumenical movement. Rather, within each profile there can be discerned an inner uncertainty about methods.

## 3.1. Dialogue

The oldest and most widespread ecumenical method is "dialogue", i.e.
a deliberately guided conversation between representatives of different
churches. In the course of time, the dialogue method has spread and been
applied to the encounter between Christians and people of other faiths or
ideologies, and also to Christian efforts to reach responsible solutions to
social and political conflicts. Particularly in these two more recent areas
of dialogue it has become clear that dialogue is more than a method or a
tool for achieving certain goals. Encounter with others in dialogue, as
opposed to polemical and aggressive confrontation, has come virtually to
be regarded as a criterion for relationships in the spirit of the gospel.
Dialogue is more than exchange of information. It is not only about
communication with the aim of reaching agreement. Dialogue is essentially a "meeting of life with life" (M. Buber). True human life is fulfilled
in dialogue. It is an expression of human community. This "material"
understanding of dialogue is in tension with the "instrumental" understanding of dialogue as a method. This tension lies behind the uncertainty
about methods in the ecumenical movement.

The following observations are limited to internal Christian dialogue on
matters of faith and order (i.e. doctrine and church order). After centuries
of reciprocal polemical separation and non-communication between the
Christian churches, the ecumenical movement has succeeded in bringing
the churches together in dialogue. Initially it was appropriate for dialogue
to be used principally as a tool to identify as clearly as possible the
differences and common ground between the traditions of the churches.
The goal of this patient conversation was to take stock, soberly and
honestly, in the hope that the area of common ground would gradually
increase. Such dialogue was only possible on the assumption that there
was as it were a spiritual communion between the separated churches
which was antecedent to all their efforts to overcome their divisions.[22]

Of course, this "comparative method", and the instrumental understanding of dialogue that went with it, after some time inevitably
discovered its limitations. The agreements aimed at in the course of this
dialogue offered no adequate firm basis for the hoped-for communion.
The "Christological change", already mentioned under the heading
"unity" as determinative of goals, led to a basically new direction in
ecumenical theological dialogue, which has come to be known as the
"Christological method". Dialogue by the churches with one another was
now understood to be an essential feature of their common journey, by
which they endeavoured to make visible the unity given in Christ which

could not be taken from them. The various traditions of the churches were brought together in open dialogue, which itself became an expression of the growing fellowship between them.

E. Schlink later described this new approach to dialogue as a "Copernican revolution":

> We do not have to compare others with ourselves, but we do have to compare ourselves together with them with the apostolic witness to Christ, and only in that way, starting with Christ, will we reach true knowledge of ourselves and others. We must learn to see ourselves, so to speak, from outside. [23]

This relativizing of the actually existing differences in doctrine and order between the churches prepared the way for a new practice of dialogue, which has proved to be extraordinarily fruitful, despite all the later justified criticism of the hermeneutically questionable unhistorical appeal to the apostolic witness to Christ. Yet this perception of the inner diversity in the biblical record frees us from the obsession that dialogue must produce complete agreement or consensus.

The active entry into the ecumenical movement of the Roman Catholic Church, together with the increased involvement of the Orthodox churches in ecumenical work, marked a real breakthrough. A new common language had to be forged and the already achieved insights and basic approaches reviewed. A document drawn up at the beginning of the cooperation of the Roman Catholic Church and the WCC, "On the Ecumenical Dialogue", [24] certainly holds the two understandings of dialogue together — the instrumental and the material, and the horizontal and the vertical. It takes up the basic Christological approach, which also found expression in the documents of the Second Vatican Council. In practice, however, there was — unnoticeably at first, and then increasingly clearly — a return to the old comparative method. This was true above all of the numerous bilateral doctrinal conversations which the Roman Catholic Church held after the Council with individual churches and Christian world communions. The premiss of all these conversations was that unity of belief is an essential condition for the unity of the church. The goal of dialogue was, by producing as wide a consensus as possible, to express this unity in belief and so create the preconditions for the achievement of unity and communion between the churches.

The understanding behind the method of these doctrinal conversations has recently been succinctly summed up in a study by the German

Ecumenical Study Committee (Deutscher Ökumenischer Studienauss-chuss, or DÖSTA) as follows:

> The starting point for doctrinal conversations is the respective *standpoint* of each confession. They discuss these standpoints in *dialogue* with the aim of reaching a *doctrinal consensus*. When this consensus is achieved, it is received in the still separated churches. When the *reception process* is completed, *communion* between the churches is restored and then the unity of the church has been achieved. [25]

By means of this method notable results have in fact been achieved. But the wider the unofficial consensus becomes, the more clearly are the limitations of this method to be seen. The transition from the dialogue stage to the reception stage does not really materialize. Rather, dialogues seem almost to reinforce confessional self-awareness. And so ever new demands and expectations are being placed on a firm consensus on the one hand, while on the other doubts are increasing as to whether it is possible at all to move from convergence to consensus. Are there not perhaps irreducible differences, which cannot be reconciled by a concep-tual linguistic formula? How much consensus is necessary as a basis for the unity of the church? Is it possible to talk of unity and communion as long as differences, inconsistencies or even contradictions remain? Can unity in belief be achieved anyway by way of doctrinal consensus? Was there ever such an overall doctrinal consensus in the ancient undivided church?

That series of questions can be prolonged indefinitely. They typify the material and methodological uncertainty which characterizes contempo-rary ecumenical debate. The number of proposed solutions formulated and put forward for discussion both by individual theologians and by ecumenical groups and commissions in recent years is so great that an overview is hardly possible. They begin with the meaning of reception or with the relation between doctrinal consensus and living in communion. They attempt to interpret dialogue and consensus as open processes, or, with reference to the concept of the "hierarchy of truths", to determine more clearly the boundaries of the unity in belief to be achieved. With the help of detailed analyses from biblical theology and the history of doctrine, the attempt is made to define more clearly the relation between unity and diversity, communion and differentness. Now and then a fundamentally dissenting thesis is advanced which leaves all at the disposal of divine providence alone. Although as a result of this intensive debate on methods the conviction is emerging that even unity in belief will be unity in diversity, the future direction which dialogue should take is still not clear.

The conclusion can be drawn that ecumenical debate once again, although with a high degree of reflection, has reached the limits of the instrumental, horizontal understanding of dialogue. Only a resolute softening of confessional positions by a common back-reference, by convergence towards the centre of the gospel, to Jesus Christ, can break through the impasse. In that case, it would have to be taken seriously that baptism and the baptismal confession of faith in Jesus Christ itself establishes that decisive communion in the body of Christ which precedes all our efforts for consensus in doctrine and order. Ecumenical dialogue would then no longer be a means to an end but the inevitable expression of communion between those who are different but who are held together, not by the same opinions or identical doctrine, but who mutually enrich one another in their diversity. This return to the centre of the gospel as the critical yardstick of all doctrine and church order was the decisive step which made it possible for the Leuenberg agreement to be concluded in 1973 between the Lutheran, Reformed and United churches of Europe.[26] The same basic methodological principle underlies the major study on the condemnations of the sixteenth century.[27] It must be admitted that, as long as this step is not taken in common, ecumenical dialogue will not escape from its present uncertainty. It is indeed a "Copernican revolution", a real ecumenical conversion that is being demanded of the churches. Will it happen?

### 3.2. Commitment to justice — but how?

The widening of the horizon of ecumenical action to the whole of humanity, the "whole inhabited earth", at the end of the 1960s, led to an increasingly acute awareness of the structural distortions in relations between North and South, rich and poor, and industrialized and developing nations. "Justice" became the central ethical category, replacing the earlier leading concept of "responsibility", which proved inappropriate for forming ethical responses to the new structural problems. So there exists today wide ecumenical agreement that commitment to justice is a direct consequence of Christian belief. However, as to the question what form this commitment to justice should take, soon after the Uppsala assembly opinions began to diverge. We meet here a further uncertainty as regards ecumenical methods.

Two differing strategies can be discerned. They are not mutually exclusive in principle, and can even complement each other. But they are expressions of different perceptions of the problem and thus often find themselves in tension or opposition. The first strategy begins from a *global* perception of the problem and is directed towards changing political, social and economic *structures*. This strategy was at the forefront in the early years after the Uppsala assembly. The ecumenical movement began to be aware in a comprehensive sense of its "world responsibility". Thus fresh tools were created to analyze the problems of global structures such as dependent development, racism, population growth, the arms race and disarmament, the influence of science and technology, limits to growth and destruction of the environment. In these analyses and in the quest for adequate solutions, close ties were built up between the initiatives of the churches in the ecumenical movement and the corresponding efforts being made within the United Nations, particularly the UN specialist agencies. Thus, for a long time, great hopes were directed towards the attempt to build a "new world economic order". There was admittedly from the beginning no lack of critics who warned against the abstractions of global analyses and their corresponding strategies. When from the mid 1970s it became clear that the attempt to build a new world order would fail, and at the same time transnational economic and financial corporations began to fill the power vacuum with structures which they controlled, it became apparent that the creation of more just structures was primarily a question of power-sharing: redistribution of power, not technical solutions to the problem.[28]

The second strategy begins from *direct experience at local level* of injustice, exploitation, oppression, discrimination and human rights violations. Its goal is *independence* and *participation* by people and societies trapped in structures of dependence. It is directed towards mobilizing and organizing those affected, so that they can become "subjects of their own history". Its field of activity is popular movements in villages and rural areas and in the slums of industrial conurbations. It is thus sceptical towards the hope of achieving a new order of international relations by means of political negotiations between representatives of governments; for it is influenced by the basic experience that even, and especially, in the poor nations of the South, their rulers seldom represent the interests and needs of the mass of the people. From this perspective, commitment to greater justice thus means above all active participation by the people in the economic and political decisions which determine their lives. It is thus appropriate to look for the practice of ecumenical solidarity as a basic requirement for action.

Both strategies are concerned to achieve greater justice in the political, economic and social realms. Both are marked by insight into the global interconnection of structures and interests, and the imbalance of power relationships. But what appears from one perspective as a complex structural problem, as a *crisis* in world structures, which must be changed and adapted to new circumstances with the help of a carefully planned, long-term strategy (e.g. the IMF), appears increasingly from the other perspective as a *struggle* simply to survive. The first strategy, in order to achieve greater justice, is concerned to ensure that the political decision-making process functions efficiently and that abuse of power is prevented by effective checks. The second strategy is sceptical towards the "normal political process" and tends to doubt the legitimacy of power structures in which those affected do not directly participate. In the first case, the principal forms of action are giving advice, making appeals and, when necessary, addressing critical protests to the decision-makers responsible. The methods used are discussion, public statements, or even mobilizing public opinion. In the second case, the main interest is in self-organization with the aim of mobilizing a countervailing power even to the point of overt resistance.[29]

The key words "force" and "violence" have been an acid test for this whole area since the Uppsala assembly, and also, unintentionally, a means of distinguishing between the two strategies. In many churches and social settings, the very words "struggle for justice" and "resistance" conjure up associations with "force" or "violence". Despite careful ecumenical analyses into the problem of violence and non-violence in the struggle for social justice and also the extraordinarily restrained recommendations for action, the different perceptions of the problem are concentrated in these two key words. Here the uncertainty regarding strategies becomes open contradiction and conflict. This is in any case inevitable, when the act of exerting political, economic or social pressure in the form of civil disobedience, boycotts or sanctions is interpreted as the use of force. Is it possible for the deliberate violation of rules to be part of a strategy to achieve greater justice?

This short examination of the issue of force and violence enables us now to make the distinction between these two methods and strategies in a different way by reference to the value of order in work for justice. Do Christians and churches have a basic responsibility for maintaining order in human society, even when that "order" is acknowledged to be unjust? Where there is, as in most of the major churches, including the Roman Catholic Church, a strong preference for order, then work for justice will concentrate on formulating Christian principles, linked with the realistic admission that these principles can seldom be put fully into practice in situations of acute social conflict. In that case, it is important that the churches do not take up sides in conflicts, but make themselves available as advocates of moderation, mediation and reconciliation. This is not only the attitude of the Roman Catholic hierarchy but also of the majority of WCC member churches, and not only in the industrialized nations with democratic constitutions. The South African Kairos document has very clearly set out the style of action of this so-called "church theology".[30]

Conversely, if one sees in conflicts about justice not only a breakdown or crisis in normal political life but rather the inevitable outcome of the intractable imbalance of domination and dependence, then maintaining the order of human society cannot — in face of its manifest disorder — be the supreme value. Then the struggle for justice and participation will consciously accept temporary intensification of disorder and remain critical of all order which can be abused as a tool of domination. This applies also, and especially, to concepts of economic and social order which claim Christian legitimation. The newly discovered biblical "option for the poor" has become the rallying cry for this form of action. It is the inspiration not only of the basic church communities in Latin America, but to an increasing extent of ecumenical action at the base in other parts of the world.

Uncertainty as to methods paralyzes the ecumenical movement's ability to act. A decision must be made. This tension has come out within the WCC particularly in connection with the Programme to Combat Racism, the study and action programme on transnational corporations, and the research on a "church in solidarity with the poor", and there is no doubt that it has also strained relations between the WCC and the Roman Catholic Church and made cooperation difficult, e.g. in connection with SODEPAX.

This conflict of strategies reaches its highest intensity where racism, nuclear weapons and deterrence, and structural poverty are seen as a challenge to the confession of the Christian faith, and consequently their rejection as a matter of belief and their Christian legitimation as heresy. Where Christians and churches feel under an obligation, for the sake of the integrity of their confession of God in Jesus Christ, to unmask unjust structures of power as the worship of false gods and to confront them with an absolute "no", then it would seem that the two strategies are no longer capable of being reconciled. But, what follows concretely for our work for justice from such an act of confession? The ecumenical movement is still far from finding a commonly agreed answer to this question. It is, however, indicative that the example of the historic peace churches, which have been committed to the ecumenical movement from the beginning, is now being taken really seriously for the first time. At the same time it is clear that this form of radical prophetic criticism has no roots in the tradition of the "catholic" churches, while it does have deep roots in the theocratic tradition of Protestantism of the Calvinist type (cf. the Confessing Church and Bonhoeffer). So, despite unambiguous statements of belief, the basic uncertainty remains.

### 3.3. Ecumenical learning — changed awareness or participation?

In recent years ecumenical learning has become the magic word for the methods of ecumenical renewal. This perspective, too, has its roots in the time of the WCC Uppsala assembly. The broadening of the ecumenical horizon beyond the Christian community to the whole of humankind, the "whole inhabited earth", was understood not least as an educational challenge. Christians and churches had to learn to break out of their provincialism and to "think globally". Since then, educational programmes have become a permanent ingredient of all ecumenical work in the areas of mission, development, peace, human rights, etc. Ernst Lange particularly, under the stimulus of the then recently initiated international debate on education and through the educational philosophy of Paulo Freire, devised a concept of ecumenical learning aimed at freeing the parochial mentality from its limitations and at participation and change. [31] Ecumenical learning in this sense is not learning information but learning experience. Decisive learning experiences take place in dealing with those conflicts in which world problems present themselves in one's everyday world. Groups in which conflicts could be simulated and acted out became an essential framework for processes of ecumenical learning. Some guidelines of the Evangelical Church in Germany dated 1985 sum up the essential features of this understanding of ecumenical learning:

> It is about crossing frontiers and involvement in action; it is about learning together with others and making connections; it includes intercultural learning and is an integrated process. [32]

Ecumenical learning was thus given a prominent position as the essential methodological key for ecumenical renewal. Indeed, the whole ecumenical movement could be understood as a comprehensive learning exercise, as an ongoing learning process! It is certainly no coincidence that this concentration on the issue of education and learning became evident precisely during the period of radical change after the Uppsala assembly. As one looks back on the debate on education in the ecumenical movement, it is in fact noticeable that the theme of education always surfaces when decisive radical changes are having to be dealt with.

There is no doubt that the impetus linked with the key words "ecumenical learning" has yielded many important insights and experiences. The task of encouraging, enabling and supporting ecumenical learning processes has in the meantime been recognized and translated into action in a variety of ways. The goal of ecumenical learning is to enable the Christian conscience, in the happy phrase of Ernst Lange, "to adjust itself to the larger household... of the whole inhabited earth". [33] But here once again, after the initial euphoria, ecumenical uncertainty has set in. Lange himself encouraged this development to a certain extent by translating the eminently social Brazilian key concept of *conscientização* (Freire) into the individualistic concept of "awareness- or consciousness-building". Is ecumenical learning a change in awareness or is it rather an active participatory process?

As originally conceived, ecumenical learning was understood as a process characterized by involvement, participation and active experience of conflict. In transplanting this insight into the regular life of the churches and the ecumenical movement a teaching method now threatened to become simply the introduction of ecumenical content into Christian education work at all levels. Ecumenical learning was developed as an educational method to transmit ecumenical awareness. The relevant church adult education programmes, and also instruction in church and school, impart information about global problems and their interconnectedness. At best, the link is also made with experiences in the learner's own context. We are told to "think globally and act locally", but the local action corresponding to global thinking is very rarely an integral element in the learning process, let alone its starting point. The areas of ecumenical learning in recent years which could have set an example, such as the South African boycott campaign by the Evangelical Women's Work in West Germany, the peace movement, and more recently the conciliar process for Justice, Peace and the Integrity of Creation, have hardly been actively taken up, but rather been institutionalized and domesticated.

By contrast with this stress on ecumenical awareness-building, in ecumenical practice particularly in the nations and churches of the southern hemisphere it has become evident that active participation is the principal key to ecumenical renewal. Such participation opens up decisive

learning opportunities for women, youth, and those hitherto marginalized. Here learning means direct empowerment for action. The basic
thesis that ecumenical learning begins with one's own experience does
not here have to be conveyed by formal teaching. Conversely, it has
become clear that ecumenical learning without participation atrophies into
transmission of information and knowledge unrelated to people's own
experiences.

The churches, and also ecumenical institutions and organizations, are
uncertain as to how it is possible to organize an open learning process
structured for change and active participation and not prone to lapse into
formalism. Is the "church as a learning community" a realistic concept of
practical ecclesiology? Does the learning strategy of ecumenical renewal
inevitably clash with ecclesiastical strategies to maintain the status quo
and to preserve continuity?

Ecumenical learning takes place in community, and thus ecumenical
communities and action groups have increasingly become the decisive
promoters of the process of ecumenical learning. The uncertainty as
regards methods thus points directly to the question as to who takes
responsibility for the ecumenical movement.

## 4. Uncertainty as to who takes responsibility for the ecumenical movement

Who are the subjects of the ecumenical movement? Who are the
movers of the movement? The above-mentioned uncertainties appear here
once again but in a different guise. Indeed, most tensions have symbolically and consciously taken the form of conflicts for their respective
influence between the various constituencies responsible for the ecumenical movement.

### 4.1. A fellowship of churches

There are first the churches. From a historical point of view, they were
not in fact the initiators of the ecumenical movement. It arose rather on
the periphery of the major churches and denominations in the area of the
various supra-confessional federations and alliances which had arisen out
of the revival movement in the previous century. A decisive role in
building the ecumenical movement was played by the World Student
Christian Federation and the cooperative associations of missionary
societies, together with the Young Men's Christian Association. Most of
the early campaigners in the ecumenical movement were equally rooted in
all these areas of work.

The later decision to make the ecumenical movement an affair of the churches themselves was the consciously drawn conclusion from the rediscovery of the church in conflicts with anti-Christian forces, particularly fascism in the 1930s. It arose from the conviction that Christian belief directly conditions the form in which the church exists and vice versa. So the World Council of Churches was founded as a "fellowship of churches" (WCC basis). Only churches were invited to become members, and not individuals or para-church associations or groups.

The decision to take that course at the founding of the WCC, which led among other things to the disbandment of the World Alliance for Promoting International Friendship through the Churches with all its rich tradition, was criticized at the time on two grounds. On the one hand, it was feared that the ecumenical movement would become paralyzed as a consequence of its being "ecclesiasticized". The same concern was voiced again later in missionary circles at the time of the unification of the International Missionary Council and the WCC. On the other hand, the danger was perceived that the WCC as the central world institution might intervene in the internal affairs of member churches. This fear became acute again in the negotiations about possible WCC membership of the Roman Catholic Church.

In the forty years since the founding of the WCC the constituted churches have slowly opened themselves to the ecumenical movement. In this respect too, the Uppsala assembly represents a qualitative leap forward: the ecumenical movement became a pan-Christian and truly worldwide movement. In the last twenty years there has been developed a close network of interchurch relations, in the form of conversations, partnerships, aid projects, regular visits and personnel exchange programmes. In most churches institutions for ecumenical relations, study, information exchange and formation have been set up. Ecumenical issues regularly appear on the agendas of church synods and church leaders' meetings. The most impressive example of this is the reception process for the convergence document on *Baptism, Eucharist and Ministry*.

Certainly in the intervening years the ecumenical movement has become an affair of the churches themselves. With that, it has also, admittedly, become an arena for church power struggles and battles for influence. In the area of international ecumenical work it is often very difficult for church representatives to keep national and church interests apart. All this has contributed to "ecclesiastical ecumenism" becoming increasingly a formal matter of interchurch relations, and particularly foreign relations. This development has been reinforced by the involvement of the Roman Catholic Church in the ecumenical movement. The cultivation of ecumenical relations now seems naturally to be a task for especially designated persons: for bishops it is part of their church leadership responsibility.

So then, is it the churches who are responsible for the ecumenical movement? They have certainly heard and heeded the call for ecumenical cooperation. But we may be permitted to ask with Ernst Lange whether they have truly incorporated it into their self-understanding as churches or whether they have simply tacked it on.[34] They have, without doubt, taken up important ecumenical initiatives and become open to one another. Interchurch relations have become a normal part of church life. Meanwhile, in many places a common ecumenical tradition has grown up. Important links in this have been joint Bible translations, liturgical texts, hymn books, education curricula, and jointly sponsored agencies.

In the normal conduct of relations, "church" means, however, in most cases the leadership of the churches. This holds good whatever the confessional tradition or geographical area. Now, church leaders have a pressing concern to keep their own church together institutionally as an integrated whole. They see their most important task as maintaining the unity of their own church. They thus promote the ecumenical movement wherever it benefits their own church; but they remain hesitant, or apply the brakes sharply, when ecumenical initiatives could disturb the inner unity of their own church or make their own members restive. They speak of the "scandal" of the division of the church, support all calls for common witness and service, but when it becomes a matter of re-examining traditional loyalties (national or confessional) so as to strengthen ecumenical fellowship and solidarity with other churches, then they often point to their own church members, who (they say) are not yet ready to go along with the steps being demanded of them! It is, in many cases, a plausible argument, but it also exactly typifies this point of ecumenical uncertainty.

## 4.2. Ecumenical organizations

At first the ecumenical movement took form organizationally in a multitude of associations and federations. These organizations, while being flexible, were only to a limited extent capable of carrying the movement, as they remained dependent on voluntary work and funding. After the founding of the WCC, its organizational form became the model for numerous similar councils at national, local and regional level. More and more of these originally voluntary ecumenical associations have united with these ecumenical councils. Like the WCC most of these councils are councils of churches. After initial hesitation the Roman Catholic Church has become a member of an increasing number of national and regional councils of churches through its corresponding geographical structures. In recent years such a council of churches has been formed in France with Roman Catholic participation, and the Roman Catholic Church is a full member of the new "ecumenical instruments" in the British Isles.

Most of these councils of churches have adopted the basic principles of the WCC constitution. In practice, however, they concentrate primarily on issues of practical church cooperation, particularly in those areas where the individual churches do not have sufficient opportunities for action.

In its Toronto statement[35] (1950) the WCC sought to clarify unambiguously its relation to the churches. It does not view itself as a "super-church" and does not claim churchly functions for itself. Its intention is to draw the churches into intensive dialogue with one another and promote cooperation between them. It thus sees itself as an instrument, a tool or servant of the churches, who themselves are responsible for the ecumenical movement. At the same time, the WCC has repeatedly described itself as "an instrument of the ecumenical movement", even as its "privileged instrument". This claim has also been expressly reaffirmed in the conversations with the Roman Catholic Church. The ecumenical movement is not identical with the WCC, but extends beyond the actually existing churches. "Instrument of the ecumenical movement" — does that mean agent for renewal and change as opposed to interest in preservation, continuity and maintaining the status quo? The ecumenical organizations are nothing without the churches, but at the same time their raison d'etre lies in calling the churches out of the parochialism of their confessional or national existence.

The WCC and its associated councils have constantly had to lay themselves open to the reproach that in their commitment and the formulation of ecumenical goals and positions they are ahead of the churches and that they are speaking and acting without the approval of the churches who are responsible for them and set them their tasks. Behind that reproach is the clear opinion that ecumenical organizations should be no more than instruments, organs carrying out the tasks and wishes which the churches have formulated. Many ecumenical organizations, influenced by this criticism, have sought to strengthen their links with the life of the churches.

Do then the ecumenical organizations have a responsibility for the ecumenical movement? They do, but only to the extent that they take it upon themselves to do more than organize and administer ecumenical relations. But, if they do, tension with the churches as those officially responsible is bound to occur. Such tension is structural in nature and largely independent of the persons involved. The picture is yet further complicated by the multiplicity of organizations with ecumenical pretensions, which are either fully dependent on the churches, such as most of the Christian world communions (world confessional bodies) or which operate without any link with the established churches, such as most organizations of evangelical tendency. The ecumenical councils are organizations *sui generis*, and therein lies their weakness and also their strength. They have to accept that other organizations, either because they are composed of the like-minded or because they are not under institutional church control, can in any case often work more effectively in the practical realm.

The ecumenical organizations are thus in no way uniquely or decisively responsible for the ecumenical movement. But, were it not for them, the impetus of the movement would soon be lost. For the movement by its nature reaches beyond the actually existing churches. The organizations are caught in a dilemma: should they be instruments of the churches or of the ecumenical movement? Success in holding the two together has always been achieved only for limited periods. Here is the root of the widespread uncertainty felt by these organizations about their place and their priorities.

### 4.3. A network of grassroots movements and action groups

Confronted by the pressing challenges of injustice, violence, oppression and the threat to survival, ecumenical grassroots or action groups have been formed in many churches in all parts of the world. These groups are either associations of those affected by these problems, who have begun to campaign together for their rights and to challenge the churches to take ecumenical action, or are expressions of the church's own commitment to them in ecumenical solidarity. Although the initiative for forming such groups has come out of ecumenical work itself, their formation has been part of the wider phenomenon of the new social movements which originated in the civil rights movement and the student movement of the 1960s.

The impetus given by the Uppsala assembly became in many churches the focal point which triggered off the formation of such groups, which in their composition broke out of the traditional, class-bound order of the church establishment. After the collapse of the former Christian students' movement, they have made a decisive contribution to mobilizing Christians at the grassroots and changing their awareness. Since then, over the last twenty years, in virtually all countries and churches there has been a great number of such groups, networks and associations which have had a determining influence on and have decisively changed the profile of the ecumenical movement.

It is a characteristic feature of these groups that they are independently organized and open to participation by all. They operate within the sphere of the church, but in most cases without institutional ties. A good number of them look to the churches or church and ecumenical institutions for organizational or financial support, and for most of them it is true that in their political or social campaigning they are dependent on the protection which church groups still enjoy in public life. This does not prevent many of them from having an extremely critical attitude to the constituted churches, although in the domain of Roman Catholicism church ties are as a rule stronger. They typically think of themselves as an "ecumenical avant-garde", advocates of the ecumenical movement within the realm of the institutional churches. This situation, allied with their open nature and undefined legal and institutional status, is the cause of the widespread strained relationships between the churches and their ecumenical groups.

Have these groups become those effectively responsible for the ecumenical movement? Many of them would regard themselves in such a way. But does this claim square with reality? Here we quickly encounter their limitations:

— Most of these groups have come into being in reaction to a particular pressing problem. They often have a clearly defined goal for their action, and disintegrate when that goal is achieved or proves to be incapable of achievement. Many of them have the character more of an open coalition than of a committed fellowship. These groups take ecumenical commitment to mean: the struggle against racism, defence of human rights, campaigning against nuclear weapons, partnership in development, or changing one's life-style. Just in the last few years networks have developed between the individual groups expressing the inherent connection between these various issues. The ecumenical women's movement has played a pioneering role in this regard.

— As a consequence of the new departures after the Second Vatican Council many ecumenical groups were formed between Christians from the Roman Catholic Church and from WCC member churches.

Most of them did not survive beyond the stage of getting to know one another, and faded away because of the lack of opportunities for active participation. In their place in recent years evangelically-oriented house groups have increasingly made their appearance. Their organizational principle is the same as that of the ecumenical groups, but their criticism of the churches also includes the ecumenical movement.

— For many of the ecumenical groups their engaging in concrete tasks and campaigns involves being prepared to enter into coalitions and to seek cooperation with other social movements which are outside the Christian, church sphere. Their interest in political alliances compels them in many cases to compromise or to forget their Christian identity and the style of action that goes with it. It thus remains an open question whether and to what extent they can claim to be a "social action arm" of the church.

— Under the influence of the "base church communities" in Latin America and other initiatives (e.g. Taizé), many of these groups are seeking a new combination of "struggle and contemplation", political action and spirituality, concrete commitment and worship. They have made a decisive contribution to breathing new life into the public aspect of Christian spirituality. However, the claim by these groups to be among those responsible for the ecumenical movement will only prove credible in the long run if they are prepared to answer this question concerning what is central to their commitment and the action which goes with it.

— The question of the church status of such groups has been the object of lively debate in recent years. The controversy in Latin America over the "church of the people" and the emergence of the church ("ecclesiogenesis") out of the life of the people has in particular reverberated far beyond that continent. It is a debate of vital importance for the future of the ecumenical movement. Ultimately it is a question of whether the ecumenical movement is an affair of the whole people of God, an integral part of the spiritual vocation of every Christian through baptism, or simply a matter of interchurch relations.

The uncertainty and mutual obstructiveness of those who consider themselves responsible for the ecumenical movement is having a paralyzing effect on its future. No one may claim a monopoly of the ecumenical movement — neither the churches, nor the ecumenical organizations, nor the groups. The hidden subject of the ecumenical movement is God, through God's Spirit. The future strength of the ecumenical movement will depend on whether the conflict between those with responsibility for it can be successfully transformed into a productive forward thrust. That does, of course, assume that all partners are prepared to think of themselves in relative terms and to trust the Spirit of God more than their own strategies.

## 5. Summary

The foregoing observations on the "uncertainty in the ecumenical movement" are intended to enable a sober stocktaking to take place. They relate almost exclusively to material from the work of the WCC. To complete the picture, they would need to be supplemented by examples from national and local ecumenical life. But completeness is not here intended, but rather the exposure of typical areas of conflict which characterize present ecumenical work. All too often these conflicts are suppressed or played down in an ecumenical balancing act.

A short time ago Werner Simpfendörfer stated with undertones of resignation that the ecumenical utopia is losing its children. After a quite long period, during which the WCC (or, at least, "Geneva") has not been spared conflicts, the impression is now gaining ground "that even 'Geneva' is at the present time no longer sure of what it is about".[36] He recalls the worldwide ecumenical vision of the Uppsala assembly, which at that time inspired so many, but he also sees the rightness of Lange's diagnosis, when he spoke of the "parochialism of consciences". Simpfendörfer has given us a sobering description of the present uncertainty of the ecumenical movement. He has perhaps underestimated the deeper roots of that uncertainty. But he concludes with the hope that there are still glowing embers among the ashes of the old utopias. That hope also lies behind my stocktaking of the situation, which is why our analysis must be taken further.

# 2. The Classical Self-understanding of the Ecumenical Movement

How are we to interpret the foregoing examples of ecumenical uncertainty? They are taken from various levels and have different backgrounds and causes, and it would be a denial of the profoundly contradictory nature of the present situation to attempt to reduce them to one common core. Similarly, the particular contrasting options cannot be simply accounted for on confessional or regional grounds, even though it is naturally tempting to do so. These tensions are to observed in one form or another in all ecumenical contexts. Finally, what we have here is not an ecumenical version of the opposing political positions of "conservatives" and "progressives".

It must not, however, be overlooked that an interpretation drawn only from within the ecumenical movement would be inadequate. The parallels and analogies are only too clear between this ecumenical uncertainty and the confusing contemporary scene as a whole, which, in the Western world at least, has been exercising the minds of people such as Jürgen Habermas for something like the past ten years.

We are living in a time of radical change, or at least of transition. Interpreters of the intellectual and social scene speak of a transition into the "post-modern" age, or they state the need for a new, "post-critical" way of thinking.

The uncertainty in the ecumenical movement, while it does have its own internal causes, can and must therefore be also interpreted against this background of deep-seated uncertainty which has seized all aspects of the hitherto prevailing constellation of human consciousness, social order, the structures of economic production and forms of political action.

## 1. Paradigm shift

To describe this situation of transition the concept of "paradigm shift" has been borrowed from the contemporary debate on the philosophy and history of science. What is meant by "paradigm shift"? In its more narrow sense a "paradigm" is a "model case" or a "prime example". With this meaning the concept has found its way into modern everyday language. But, in addition, a further meaning has developed in which "paradigm" is taken to signify "a guiding frame of reference which gives direction and criteria for human intellectual activity".[1] The American philosopher of science Thomas Kuhn, who has placed the concept in this dual sense at the centre of his analyses, defines particularly the second level of meaning — which is what especially concerns us here — as follows:

> [The term "paradigm"] stands for the entire constellation of beliefs, values, techniques, and so on shared by the members of a given community.[2]

Kuhn's interest is in the development of scientific knowledge. He interprets "normal science" as the activity devoted to solving specific scientific problems. In doing so, it follows generally recognized rules, which are legitimated for it by an all-inclusive paradigm. If, in the course of scientific investigation, anomalies are observed or discoveries made which cannot be explained by the rules in force, i.e. the generally accepted scientific laws, then fresh scientific theories are formed, which may ultimately even lead to a crisis of confidence in the paradigm. The crisis reaches its conclusion when a changed paradigm emerges, which again functions as a general framework of orientation and both incorporates the new theories and confirms the claims to validity of the former paradigm within newly defined boundaries. The most impressive examples of such an overall paradigm shift are the transition from Ptolomaic to Copernican cosmology and the replacement of classic Newtonian physics in this century by the theory of relativity and quantum physics.

The debate on Kuhn's theses on the history and philosophy of scientific theory cannot and should not be gone into here. They have, however, provoked widespread discussion, not least because they have established the principle that scientific knowledge even in the natural sciences is historical in nature. In particular, in the interpretative disciplines of the humanities and the social sciences, Kuhn's theses have been taken up with interest. They have also gained ground in fundamental philosophical thought in the realm of the natural sciences.

As long as the confusing situation remains unresolved, talk of a paradigm shift is hypothetical in nature. Only with hindsight can it be seen whether a hitherto leading frame of reference has been replaced by a qualitatively new one. If, however, the perception of reality in particular areas becomes a matter of controversy, it is of decisive importance whether the perceived crisis is understood as an irregularity or a limited departure from the accepted norms and rules, or whether it represents a challenge to the currently valid framework of thought and action. In the first case, it is sufficient to correct, adapt and develop the known laws, theories or rules; in the second case, a qualitatively new beginning is demanded. In the social and political field this distinction is designated by the concepts of "evolution" and "revolution". What is decisive for us to be able to talk of the need for a "paradigm shift", or of its already happening, is not whether a ready-made conclusive alternative can already be set over against the hitherto leading normative frame of reference, but that it is being fundamentally challenged from more and more sides.

Talk of a "paradigm shift" in contemporary intellectual debate is closely linked with a particular interpretation of the content of the changes taking place. Because of this, the primarily epistemological and methodological thrust of Kuhn's theses runs the risk of being ignored.

The following exposition thus holds fast to the hypothetical nature of any talk of a "paradigm shift". However, if one starts from this hypothesis of an incipient change in the basic intellectual frame of reference, then the crises in many areas appear in a different light. Then they are not so much signs of decline and disintegration but rather indications of an unconscious search. That would result in a broadening of restricted perceptive capability, a departure from the frantic concern with overcoming crises and solving problems, and would free us to concentrate on reformulating questions and examining the causes of the present crisis. The thesis of "paradigm shift" will be used in this sense in what follows to interpret the uncertainty of the ecumenical movement.

## 2. The "oikoumene" as a theological paradigm: a paradigm shift in the ecumenical movement?

To speak of "paradigm shift" in the ecumenical movement may sound like trendy jargon. It can in fact be asked whether in the more recent history of the ecumenical movement there has ever been one generally accepted paradigm for the theory and practice of ecumenism. The various profiles of the original movements which gave rise to the present institutional framework of the WCC are still, it seems, discernible. And the different confessional traditions have still today their own entry points and contacts with the ecumenical life of the church. On the other hand, there is, or at least was, some evidence of an ecumenical paradigm, which was taken for granted, and which could appeal to a basic fund of common beliefs, values and modes of behaviour. It is precisely this which is being challenged in this period of uncertainty. Conflicts, believed to be long since resolved, suddenly break out again. Here the thesis of a paradigm shift could provide some clarification, in that it enables us to see developments, which in comparison with earlier visions and hopes can only be viewed as indications of stagnation or even regression, in a new perspective as phenomena accompanying a painful transition to a new frame of reference and thought.

This replacement of a hitherto leading frame of thought by a new one is certainly a well-known and repeatedly observed process in an historical examination of the development of the ecumenical movement. This is hardly surprising, in that the ecumenical movement has been very closely interwoven with the crises and shocks accompanying growth which have marked the emergence of the modern age since the middle of the nineteenth century. A few indications will suffice to describe this interaction, among which the two critical periods of rapid change following the two world wars in this century particularly stand out.

The roots of the ecumenical movement reach back to the time when bourgeois society was developing with the industrialization of Europe and America. Colonialism and Christian mission were parallel forms of expression, at times in tension with each other, of the missionary consciousness of this society, which felt itself called to convey to the rest of humanity the blessings of Western (i.e. bourgeois) Christian civilization. The whole of humanity was viewed as a "brotherhood" under the "fatherhood of God". In this climate of "liberal internationalism" at the end of the nineteenth century, the first initiatives were taken in the direction of dialogue and cooperation between the churches, based on the conviction that there was a spiritual unity in Christendom, and an overall unity in Christian civilization. The slogan "the evangelization of the world in this generation" emphasizes the missionary consciousness of this early movement, in which genuine missionary and evangelistic motives were inextricably combined with cultural and social motives.

The first world war and its aftermath represented the first deep crisis, which also stimulated fresh initiatives. Wide cracks had become evident in the old order. The collapse of the former balance of power in Europe with the end of the great imperial monarchies, the Russian revolution, the increasing secularization of society, the world economic crisis and finally the emergence of fascism — all made this period a time of constant crisis. The framework which the ecumenical movement had used to establish its course began to break up. The liberalism of the "social gospel" was no more equal to the challenge than the internationalism of the League of Nations and its concomitant World Alliance for Promoting International Friendship through the Churches. This shaking of the foundations, which was early perceived by dialectical theology, produced a reaction in the ecumenical movement. The ancient synthesis of Christianity and (Western) culture began to disintegrate. Thus in the major ecumenical conferences in 1937 and 1938 in Oxford, Edinburgh and Tambaram, the question of the church, reflection on what it meant to be the church became central to the ecumenical paradigm, which was taking on a clear outline in the struggle against the pseudo-religious demonic powers of the totalitarian state.

As we look back, the crisis between the two world wars now appears as but the prelude to the greater shaking of the foundations after the end of the second world war. The years 1945-48 saw not only the final collapse of the old order in Europe, but also the division of the world into the spheres of influence and hegemony of the two great powers, the USA and the USSR. Far-seeing ecumenical personalities, such as Josef Hromadka, saw in this crisis the final end of the Constantinian age, i.e. a break with the age-long association of Christianity with European culture. The decisive shock for the ecumenical movement came, it must be said, only with the victory of the communist revolution in China, which put an end to the most ambitious missionary enterprise in modern Christian missionary history, and with the Korean war. Together with the successful liberation struggles in India and Indonesia, these events signalled the end of the long period of Western (Christian) world domination.

The ecumenical movement reacted to this profound crisis in its self-understanding by intense theological reflection on itself, which led to a fresh interpretation of history in the light of God's plan of salvation for humankind. The fresh understanding of the missionary calling of the church as participation in the *missio Dei*, the Christological and Trinitarian foundation of the unity of the church as "God's gift and our task", and the interpretation of the processes of rapid social change as a challenge to the churches to participate in God's action in history — all these resulted in a changed perception of ecumenism with wider horizons. The "Christian world" gave way to a vision which sought to understand the human condition from the perspective of the universal history of salvation. Thus, the "spatial" framework of thought of the earlier paradigm, which was directed to discerning and maintaining "order", was replaced by an historical framework.

## 3. The rediscovery of Christocentric universalism

We thus reach the point which set the dominant ecumenical paradigm for the following period: "world history" is understood as salvation event in the light of God's definitive action in Jesus Christ. Willem A. Visser 't Hooft, for many years the general secretary of the WCC, later coined the concept of "Christocentric universalism" to describe this frame of reference.[3] For him, the development of the ecumenical movement from its beginnings in the missionary movement in the nineteenth century until the mature expression of its self-understanding at the third assembly in New Delhi in 1961 can be interpreted as a gradual rediscovery of this specifically Christian universalism.

In a lecture given in 1962 Visser 't Hooft traces this development. Because of its characteristic emphases I shall here briefly summarize his analysis.[4] The missionary movement, at least since Edinburgh 1910, is viewed by Visser 't Hooft as deeply aware of its obligation to witness to "the world-embracing nature of the Christian faith", and of "the one urgent Christian task" of "the worldwide evangelization of the whole world". This thrust was complemented by the Faith and Order movement, which set itself the task of clarifying the nature of the unity of the universal people of God. The invitation to one of the early world conferences on issues of Faith and Order was addressed to churches "which accept our Lord Jesus Christ as God and Saviour". Later clarifications of this basic position clearly show that the movement was from the beginning guided by a Christocentric understanding of the unity of the church.

> We can only be grateful for their insistence that the unity and universality with which the ecumenical movement must be concerned can only be the one that is created by Jesus Christ himself as the one in whom God reconciles the world to himself.
>
> Just as the historic deed of the fathers of Edinburgh had been to give a clear, concrete witness to the objective of universalism — the proclamation of salvation in Christ to all men — so the fathers of Faith and Order gave a definite witness to its centre, the one Jesus Christ who is the author of both unity and universality.[5]

Even this testimony was, however, still incomplete, for in dealing with issues of church unity it would be easy to forget the objective of that unity, "in the context of the universal work of Christ in and for mankind". So in the Life and Work movement a third aspect of Christian universalism came to the fore: the proclamation of "the lordship of Christ in all realms of life".[6] The critical struggles of the 1930s led further to the recognition

> that the ecumenical movement would have to be definitely Christocentric, that it would have to be a movement of rediscovery and renewal of the church, but not of the church as an aim in itself, rather of the church as the chosen instrument for the world-embracing saving work of Christ.[7]

Visser 't Hooft continues his analysis by examining the decision to found the WCC, the reasoning behind the basis, the clarification of the ecclesiological significance of the WCC in the Toronto statement, and concludes with the completion of the process with the integration of the WCC and the International Missionary Council (IMC) and the expansion of the basis at the New Delhi assembly.

> Thus by the time of the New Delhi assembly the Council had been led step by step to work out the full implications of a specifically Christian universalism: the rootage in the common confession of the one Saviour, the concern for the unity and obedience of his people, the calling to bring the word of salvation and the ministry of reconciliation to all men everywhere.[8]

This overview by Visser 't Hooft clearly distinguishes three elements in Christocentric universalism which had emerged in their respective contexts: the confession of Jesus Christ, the unity of his people, and the call to witness and service to the whole of humankind. This overview, or review, from the year 1962 does, of course, give the impression of a consistent organic progression and passes over the decisive new direction which the ecumenical movement had taken under the influence of the collapse of the old order after the second world war, i.e. its orientation to history as a basic category of the ecumenical paradigm. This aspect thus requires further elucidation for the sake of clearer understanding. In doing this, I shall develop and give reasons for the statements at the end of the previous section.

The *first* decisive impulse came out of debates within the International Missionary Council. In the years 1947-52 the Council developed an essentially new understanding of mission. The changed world situation, particularly after the catastrophic end to missionary work in China, demanded fresh biblical and theological reflection in the light of the dominant interest in a theological interpretation of history. How could God's action in history be understood? It is here that studies from earlier years in Germany, Britain, the Netherlands and the USA bore fruit.

Despite differing emphases, they all converged in an understanding of mission as salvation history and eschatological event. The earlier liberal enthusiasm for progress was replaced by orientation to God's universal plan of salvation.

Anticipations of this fresh orientation crystallized at the meeting of the International Missionary Council in Willingen in 1952. In the concluding statement of that conference on "The Missionary Calling of the Church", the conviction is clearly expressed that mission is not an activity originating in the church but is in the first place God's action.

> The missionary movement of which we are a part has its source in the Triune God himself... God sends forth the church to carry out his work to the ends of the earth, to all nations, and to the end of time...

The church, as the pilgrim people of God, is called by God to set out on a journey and

> to go forth... to the task of bringing all things into captivity to him, and of preparing the whole earth for the day of his coming.[9]

This new definition of the nature of mission, which has since then been designated by the phrase "missio Dei", marks the transition to thinking in terms of salvation history. The whole world is understood as within the perspective of the coming kingdom of God. In the light of God's saving action in history church and mission thus belong indissolubly together. Similarly, the WCC central committee had already indicated two years previously in its statement "The Calling of the Church to Mission and to Unity" (Rolle, 1951) that it is only correct to speak of ecumenism when what is under consideration is the unity of the church and mission to the whole world. It emphasizes that

> this word, which comes from the Greek word for the whole inhabited earth, is properly used to describe everything that relates to the whole task of the whole church to bring the gospel to the whole world. It therefore covers equally the missionary movement and the movement towards unity, and must not be used to describe the latter in contradistinction to the former.[10]

This concern for salvation history is developed with particular emphasis in the report of the advisory committee for the main theme of the WCC second assembly in Evanston in 1954: "Christ, the Hope of the World".[11]

The *second* important impulse arose out of the work of the Faith and Order movement. Here the issue of the nature of the church had been a central concern since the Edinburgh world conference in 1937. Careful comparison of the various ecclesiological traditions had, however, led the Amsterdam assembly to declare that "our deepest difference", that between "Catholic" and "Protestant", could not be overcome at that time. [12]

Like the Willingen meeting in 1952 for the ecumenical understanding of mission, the third world Faith and Order conference in Lund, also in 1952, similarly marked an important advance in ecumenical work on the issue of the unity of the church. In its "Word to the Churches" the conference gives an account of this changed outlook:

> We have seen clearly that we can make no real advance towards unity if we only compare our several conceptions of the nature of the church and the traditions in which they are embodied. But once again it has been proved true that as we seek to draw closer to Christ we come closer to one another. We need, therefore, to penetrate behind our divisions to a deeper and richer understanding of the mystery of the God-given union of Christ with his church. We need increasingly to realize that the separate histories of our churches find their full meaning only if seen in the perspective of God's dealings with his whole people. [13]

The full significance, however, of this fresh orientation only became apparent in the course of further work, particularly in the study on "Christ and the Church". [14] The unity statement by the New Delhi assembly is the mature fruit of this attempt to incorporate the issue of the unity of the church into the total context of God's work from creation onwards, through the incarnation, and up to the gift of the Spirit. This change to a Christological salvation history had been prepared for by the theology of Karl Barth, while at the same time it takes up central themes in the Anglican and Orthodox traditions. Basically, it brings into sharper focus the WCC basis and its Christocentric orientation.

The *third* trail leads us back to the time of the struggle against fascism, not only in Germany but also in the occupied countries such as Norway and the Netherlands. The ecumenical movement was deeply involved in this struggle. It was against this background that Visser 't Hooft published in 1948 a series of lectures he had given one year previously under the title "The Kingship of Christ: An Interpretation of Recent European Theology". [15] In it he examines the changes in this theme in the history of the churches of the Reformation, outlines its rediscovery at the time of the church struggle, develops its biblical basis and then in two programmatic chapters draws out the consequences in the light of Christ's lordship in the church and the world. This belief in the universal lordship of Christ was so decisive for George Bell, bishop of Chichester and first moderator of the WCC central committee, that he entitled his short history of the ecumenical movement published in 1954 *The Kingship of Christ*. He sees the ecumenical movement as a movement towards recovering the fellowship of the church and aware of its obligation "to proclaim the message of the kingship of Christ, and the meaning of that kingship in action".[16]

The World Council itself made this concern for the lordship of Christ the subject of a comprehensive biblical and theological study programme following the second assembly in Evanston in 1954.[17] The following extract from the final report of this study programme will serve to give a summary of its findings:

> 1. The New Testament affirms that Jesus Christ is Lord of heaven and earth (Matt. 28:18). In him the word of God which creates and rules the world became incarnate, and God himself, the Creator and Lord of heaven and earth, is revealed in him (John 1:14; Col. 2:9). He is Lord by virtue of his passing through humiliation, suffering and death to his exaltation (Phil. 2:6-11; John 12:24).
>
> 2. The Lordship given to Christ by God will find its consummation in the day of judgment and fulfilment (1 Cor. 15:24ff.; Rev. 11:15). But as God's promise and gift it is even now already real, present, unlimited and complete, whether men acknowledge it or not (Eph. 1:20-22; Col. 2:10; 1 Tim. 3:16; 1 Pet. 3:22).
>
> 3. Christ's Lordship calls for acknowledgment by mankind, and without such acknowledgment there is no true wellbeing and salvation for the world. Wherever God brings about the miracle of faith, this acknowledgment of the hidden Lordship of Christ is evoked (Luke 10:23; John 20:29; 1 Cor. 2:9).
>
> 4. Christ's Lordship over the world finds particular manifestation in his Lordship over the church; those in the world whom Christ gathers together through the proclamation of his Lordship and the miracle of faith constitute the church. Through baptism and the eucharist he brings men to participate in his own death and resurrection in their full historical reality and uniqueness. In the church, thus brought into being, he manifests his Lordship through the Holy Spirit by leading it along his own way of suffering (Mark 8:31,34; 2 Cor. 4:10; Rev. 12:11), by displaying his strength in its weakness (2 Cor. 12:9, cf. 4:7), by bringing about obedience to the faith (Rom. 1:5), and by his real presence in its worship and sacraments (Matt. 18:20; Eph. 5:26ff.). By its very existence the church proclaims to the whole creation that the world stands under the Lordship of Christ (Matt. 5:14; Eph. 3:10).[18]

After examining in chapter two the New Testament witness to the powers in opposition to Christ's lordship, the study continues with reflection on the ways in which Christ's lordship is exercised in the area of tension between church and world, and comes to the conclusion:

> Christ's Lordship over church and world provides the proper basis for a Christian social ethic... In every situation the Lord of the world is actively at work exercising his sovereignty over nations and peoples.[19]

## 4. Christocentric universalism as the ecumenical paradigm

We have thus identified the origins and processes which led to the development of Christocentric universalism as the paradigm for the ecumenical movement. We must now fill out this review of historical origins by a more precise examination of the basic elements of the paradigm, which — independently of their original context — are closely inter-related. These basic elements have emerged as: the *Christocentric* orientation, concentration on the *church*, a *universal perspective*, and *history* as the central category of thought. The singling out of these basic elements is, of course, the result of a thematic analysis which draws on the previously mentioned texts for the purpose of interpretation.

I shall now develop and review this analysis in two stages.

First of all, I shall attempt to delineate the inner theological profile of the paradigm. Where do the emphases lie? Since that involves a systematic reconstruction, which to a certain extent remains hypothetical, I shall, secondly, in the following section, attempt an examination of how the paradigm has been used in projects and debate within the ecumenical movement. What perception of the reality of church and world has resulted from the paradigm? In both stages, I shall use the fourfold structure of the paradigm to articulate my train of thought.

### 4.1. Christocentrism

The all-determining central element in the paradigm is a deliberate *Christocentrism*. This was emphasized by Visser 't Hooft on many occasions with its programmatic implications. "The World Council of Churches is either a Christocentric movement or it is nothing at all."[20]

That sentence from his general secretary's report to the third assembly in New Delhi in 1961 was repeated some years later almost word for word, but in a different situation. Visser 't Hooft is referring to the Decree on Ecumenism of the Second Vatican Council and more particularly to the mention in it of the "hierarchy of truths".[21] He sees in the reference to the "foundation of the Christian faith" a welcome confirmation of the basic ecumenical conviction that Jesus Christ is this centre.

> I am convinced that the whole future of ecumenism depends on our faithfulness to this basic principle. The ecumenical movement is Christocentric, or it is nothing at all.... [22]

Christocentrism thus forms one of the important bridges for participation by the Roman Catholic Church in the ecumenical movement. We have, moreover, already seen that this Christological emphasis had been incorporated in the WCC basis. The intention and significance of this deliberate emphasis can most easily be demonstrated from the context of the discussions on the wording of the basis. [23] The basis speaks of Jesus Christ as "God and Saviour". This unusual wording has its origin in two different sources: the "revivalist" tradition of the Young Men's Christian Associations (Paris basis, 1855) and the high-church tradition of Anglicanism (letter of invitation of the Episcopal Church, 1911). In both cases, the wording arose out of the intention to strengthen and defend the simple biblical witness to Jesus Christ against dogmatic indifferentism and liberal credal reductionism. Its concern was to express a positive Christology without unnecessary dogmatic refinements, but including Trinitarian belief and a recognition of the true humanity of Jesus Christ. The apologetic interest was not in the human person of Jesus of Nazareth but in belief in the second person of the divine Trinity. This same concern also later ensured that the basis of the Faith and Order movement was taken over into the WCC constitution. This decision, which was by no means a foregone conclusion in the face of the liberal background of important circles in the Life and Work movement, reflects the conviction that the World Council needs a strong foundation in view of the challenge posed by pseudo-Christian theologies and ideological confusion. The reasons for this decision are summarized in a memorandum drawn up by Archbishop William Temple and sent out with the invitation to all churches to become members. It reads:

> [The Council] stands on faith in our Lord Jesus Christ as God and Saviour. As its brevity shows, the basis is an affirmation of the Christian faith of the participating churches, and not a credal test to judge churches or persons. It is an affirmation of the incarnation and the atonement. The Council desires to be a fellowship of those churches which accept these truths. [24]

In a study of the significance of Christology for the ecumenical movement, Geiko Müller-Fahrenholz emphasizes the summary dogmatic nature of the Christological statements in these ecumenical texts. [25] Any critical distinction between the differing types of New Testament Christ-ology is in fact avoided. The ecumenical texts are informed by a Christology "from above" in which the perspective "from below", the activity and preaching by the historical Jesus of Nazareth, clearly takes second place. But also, among the various types of kerygmatic Christol-ogy, a particular emphasis is consciously or implicitly made: as Müller-Fahrenholz demonstrates, the "incarnational" and the "cosmocrator" motifs are to the fore,[26] whereas by contrast the "cross motif", confession of the saving significance of the death of Jesus "for us", the cross as a sign of God's judgment on human sin, recedes into the background.[27] A glance at the New Testament texts drawn on in the ecumenical documents confirms this observation: apart from the prologue to John's Gospel, the hymn-like passages from Philippians, Colossians, Ephesians, Hebrews and Timothy are those most frequently quoted.

The influence of the Anglican and Orthodox traditions in particular finds expression in the incarnation motif, in which both follow the dominant emphasis of the Christology of the ancient church. In it either the soteriological (and ecclesiological, see below) concern comes to the fore, i.e. the divine incarnation in Jesus Christ opens up the way to sharing in the divine reality; or the universal-human concern is predomin-ant, e.g. in the Adam/Christ typology (Rom. 5:12ff.), in which the incarnation is the beginning of the new humanity. In both cases stress is laid on the real ontological union of the divine and human natures.

The "cosmocrator" motif has its roots in the primitive Christian belief that sees the resurrection of Jesus Christ as his exaltation and enthrone-ment as lord and judge of the world. This messianic Christology, which was originally linked with the apocalyptic eschatological expectation of Christ's near return to judge the nations, became detached from its eschatological setting as the expectation of its nearness faded. In early Christian hymns and credal doxologies it was linked with Christ's mediating role in creation and so becomes cosmological in scale: the exalted Christ is already lord over all principalities and powers.

Both motifs are closely related to each other in ecumenical Christol-ogy, although their distinctive emphases remain discernible. But they converge in their over-riding concern with the universal significance of the Christ event.

## 4.2. *Concentration on the church*

Concentration on the church corresponds to this Christocentric approach of the ecumenical paradigm. In Visser 't Hooft's analysis the argument for Christocentrism clearly reveals this ecclesiological concern. Just as in Christology stress is laid on the true union of God and humankind, God and the world in Jesus Christ — in contrast to the abiding distinction between them — so also in ecclesiology stress is laid on the true bond and union between Christ and his church as the foundation for the church's visible unity. This linking of Christology and ecclesiology is of decisive importance for the paradigm. In the major study on "Christ and the Church"[28] it was developed in detail: in it, the image of Christ is to the fore, either as the head of the body or as lord and ruler of his people.

This points to a possible difference in ecclesiology corresponding to the distinctive emphases of the incarnation motif and the "cosmocrator" motif. In the incarnational approach, stress is laid on the essential unity between Christ and his church on the basis of the incarnation, which results in a sacramental ecclesiology: the church in its unity becomes itself the visible embodiment of the new divine-human reality. In the "cosmocrator" approach, the church is seen as the people whom Christ, enthroned as lord and ruler of the whole world, gathers to himself: it is sent out as a witness to proclaim the lordship of Christ to all the world. Indeed, Christ uses the church as an instrument to establish his universal rule. This functional ecclesiology, which appears above all in discussion on mission and then later in debates on social ethics, avoids all statements on the nature of the church, and accords to the church simply the nature of an instrument in God's historical work in mission and salvation. It is, none the less, like sacramental ecclesiology, equally based on a deliberately Christological foundation.

## 4.3. The universal perspective

The internal tension between these two approaches, which is also apparent in the documents of the Second Vatican Council and particularly in post-conciliar debate, was resolved by the *universal perspective* of the paradigm. The concentration on the church was in fact a direct consequence of belief in the universal significance of the Christ event. The new creation in Christ, his absolute claim to lordship over all areas of life, had to be empirically visible, verifiable in history. This rediscovery of the church, in the form in which it developed particularly in ecumenical debate in the 1930s, was as yet no guarantee of an authentic Christian universalism. Both sacramental and "Christocratic" ecclesiologies can lead to a strengthening of Christian exclusivism, to attitudes and practices which not only draw a distinction between church and world but actually separate them, or make Christ's claim to lordship over church and world into a claim to power and superiority over humankind by a particular Christian culture.[29] The brief historical notes in the preceding section have demonstrated that the paradigm of Christocentric universalism came into being when the ecumenical movement was under the necessity of finding a new foundation after the collapse of the ancient synthesis of the "corpus Christianum", i.e. Christian civilization in Western countries and its universal missionary consciousness.

The following extracts from Visser 't Hooft's opening address to the Conference of European Churches in 1964 serve to underline this point:

> Europe is the one continent which can be described as an ex-corpus Christianum... The churches are still largely concerned with the conserving of the remains of the old Christian culture. There is a nostalgia for the old Christian Europe. But the finale of the symphony between Christianity and European culture is being played. We must face the new Europe and the new world, which as Bonhoeffer and now also van Leeuwen have shown us is a "mündige Welt", a world that has grown up and stands on its own feet... The churches must in this situation give up any remaining dreams concerning privilege or power. There is no way back to the corpus Christianum... Our task is therefore vastly greater than the conservation of the remnants of traditional Christendom or the calling of a few individuals out of the world into the church... And we must raise everywhere the question of the meaning of history. For the great paradox is that Europe, which brought to the whole wide world the message that history has a meaning, is also the continent where the meaning of history is most sharply called in question.[30]

## 4.4. History as the central category of thought

The experience of secularization thus made necessary a critical revision of all forms of Christian universalism marked by the static concept of a "Christian world", a "Christian order", or the institutional antithesis of church and world. Here the introduction of *history* as the central category of thought proves fruitful. The tension between the manifest particularity of the existence of the church — and, even more, the historical particularity of the Christ event — and the universal claim which the church links with its confession of faith and its existence can only be resolved within the perspective of an historical context understood eschatologically. The dynamic conception of universal history as realizing God's plan of salvation is thus the decisive link in the chain holding the basic elements of the paradigm together in tension.

For a detailed treatment, reference can again be made to the study by Müller-Fahrenholz, in which he examines the background and origins of the salvation history approach, particularly in the theological and ecclesiological work of the WCC.[31] The separate developments in missiological thinking referred to above here recede into the background. In a series of biographical theological profiles, Müller-Fahrenholz identifies the influences on the development of the salvation history approach in ecumenical debate exerted by the Anglican theologians William Temple and Leonard Hodgson on the one hand and Oscar Cullmann on the other. He also demonstrates that reflection on salvation history, and also Christocentrism, has been one of the decisive bridges of understanding between conciliar Catholicism and the ecumenical movement.[32]

Beginning with a theology of history which was developed at an ecumenical consultation on "The Meaning of History" in 1949, Müller-Fahrenholz demonstrates that ecumenical debate at the Amsterdam assembly began with a salvation history approach with a strong eschatological emphasis. In the worldwide realization of God's plan of salvation the churches have an eschatologically decisive task. Stress is placed on the "special" salvation history, oriented to the church, within the general history of God's rule from creation to its consummation. The document on the main theme of the Evanston assembly also works within this framework. It begins with a

> special (biblical) history of salvation, which has hermeneutical relevance for history in general, while the critical questions [of the assembly statement on this report] are more strongly determined by the quest for a universal history of salvation which also embraces other faiths.[33]

This trend to universalizing the salvation history approach, at the expense of giving up the eschatological dimension, continues in later debate. The Christological cosmocrator motif, belief in the universal lordship of Jesus Christ, serves as a reference point:

> The function of such a universal vision of salvation history is above all to show the obedience of faith to the cosmic Christ. But this confession at the same time shows its ecclesiological relevance: for, if there is only one cosmocrator, there can only be one oikoumene. It should thus not be overlooked that the function of the salvation history approach also consists in witnessing to the world the full solidarity of all Christians.[34]

## 5. The ecumenical movement as an expression of Christocentric universalism

The decisive contours of the ecumenical paradigm became clear when the third assembly of the WCC met in New Delhi in 1961. A series of factors combined to make this assembly the occasion when the ecumenical movement entered upon the phase of universality. It was the first assembly not to take place in one of the countries of the Western world. India symbolized the beginning of the decolonization process and the development of a humane society under democratic auspices — the opposite of communist China. Despite the great hopes surrounding church union in South India, the Indian churches lived as a small minority in an environment where Hinduism was a dominant feature, but in the 1950s they had made decisive contributions to ecumenical debate. The interest in an ecumenical interpretation of history had particularly here fallen on very fertile ground. At the New Delhi assembly the union took place between the World Council of Churches and the International Missionary Council and all its associated missionary agencies and Christian councils, particularly in Asia and Africa. The so-called "younger churches" now entered the ecumenical movement as equal partners. The theological clarification achieved in the forming of the paradigm had been an important precondition for this step. Lastly, in New Delhi the Russian Orthodox Church, together with some other Orthodox churches in countries in Eastern Europe, was received into the WCC, and for the first time official observers from the Roman Catholic Church took part in an assembly.

Thus in effect a new phase began: the ecumenical movement was from then on a movement of Christocentric universalism. How has this perspective affected our perception of church and world in subsequent years?

The following observations are limited to pursuing developments in the theological understanding of history by examining some influential study programmes and statements from the time up to the Uppsala assembly. What was the role played by the basic elements of the paradigm in the main areas of work in theology and missiology in the ecumenical movement?

My first reference is to the address given by the American Lutheran theologian Joseph Sittler at New Delhi on the theme "Called to Unity".[35] It was this address which — independently of simultaneous developments in Catholic theology by Teilhard de Chardin and others — made the phrase "the cosmic Christ" known in the ecumenical movement. Beginning with the hymn to Christ in Colossians 1:15-20 Sittler developed in his address the vision of a *cosmic Christology*. As the one who now rules, Jesus Christ is not only lord of the church and the world, but is the centre of the whole cosmos. Study in the history of doctrine and patristics had recalled the strong central position occupied by the universal dimension of God's work of reconciliation in Jesus Christ in the theology of the ancient church. Irenaeus of Lyon in particular is not only the original source of salvation history thought, but in debate with the dualistic ideas of his gnostic opponents he developed a comprehensive understanding of the universal significance of Jesus Christ. Sittler goes on to say that redemption in Christ does not concern the individual alone, nor is it limited to a particular history of salvation, but it also includes nature and the whole created cosmos.

This address by Sittler exerted at first a continuing unconscious influence. From 1964 to 1967, however, it was taken up in a study by the Commission on Faith and Order, the report of which was published in 1967 under the title "God in Nature and History".[36] As a member of the Commission, Sittler was directly involved in the planning and execution of the study programme.

The study represents an initial attempt in ecumenical debate to enter into dialogue with modern natural science and its world-view. With its historical theological approach it does not find it difficult to see a correspondence between the scientific theory of evolution and the biblical understanding of nature as creation, i.e. as an expression of God's action in history. The study takes up the language of the hymns to Christ in Ephesians and Colossians (cf. also John 1 and Heb. 1), and speaks of Jesus Christ as the mediator and perfecter of creation, the beginning of a new humanity. Humankind is fully a part of nature, i.e. is created by God and at the same time called to be responsible for the created world.

It is particularly important to note how the study takes up the development towards the increasing social, technological and economic interdependence of all parts of the world. It acknowledges that the church is caught up in this process. It understands the trend to increasing universality, not indeed as a direct consequence of the universal Christian message, but it is convinced that it is possible in this situation to witness clearly to the universal faith. It explicitly rejects any separation of salvation history and secular history and challenges all Christians to test the signs of the times in the light of their universal belief.

> God calls us to make our decisions, in the light of his coming kingdom, against hunger, suffering, poverty, discrimination and oppression, and for welfare, freedom, equality and brotherhood. The Christian has to know for himself where he sees the forces of the Spirit at work, in order that he may join them, and where he sees the forces of darkness at work, in order that he may resist them.[37]

Where the paradigm is expanded to cosmic dimensions — as in Sittler's address and in this study — the church tends to sink into the background, and even the contradictions and ambiguities of historical experience appear only peripherally. Correspondingly, the eschatological dimension of biblical historical thought hardly has a role. The question of *history* as a central category of thought was taken up instead by the Dutch Reformed theologian Arend Th. van Leeuwen in his influential book *Christianity in World History: The Meeting of the Faiths of East and West*.[38] This book is as it were a test case to discover whether the paradigm is really capable of giving an answer to the problems which this comprehensive new theological approach had unleashed. Van Leeuwen sees the process of secularization not so much as the decline of Christian civilization but rather as the completion of the process of desacralization of structures in the natural and social order which began in ancient Israel. Israel was the first to have before it the choice between "ontocracy", i.e. rule by a cosmic order permeating all things and embodied in sacral kingship, and "theocracy", i.e. God's absolute rule in history. In secularization — which he follows Friedrich Gogarten in describing as "the historicization of human existence" — the process of overcoming ontocratic structures which began in Israel is reaching its ultimate conclusion and is now turning against the "religious elements" in Christianity itself.

According to van Leeuwen we are at the end of an age, at the transition from the "Vasco da Gama era" into the "planetary world". This "planetary world" will inevitably take the form of Western technocratic civilization. It should thus be the aim of Christian mission to prepare non-Western societies spiritually and materially for this civilization. For this purpose, a truly "ecumenical theology of history" is indeed necessary, which will do for our age and the transition now taking place what Augustine's theology did at the end of the classical Mediterranean world, i.e. give a fresh interpretation of history in the light of its goal.

The insights of this "epoch-making book" (M.M. Thomas), much read in its day, were not directly taken up into the debate, although traces of them are to be found in the preparations for the Geneva conference of 1966. Of more immediate effect was the ecumenical study programme carried out in the same period on "The Missionary Structure of the Congregation", the report of which was published in 1967 under the title *The Church for Others and the Church for the World*.[39] The central concern of the study is likewise the problem of secularization in the sense of the historicization of the world as a whole. Here too secularization is seen as a fruit of the biblical witness. The God of the Bible is a God of history, of change. God changes the world in the direction of its final goal, the establishment of the divine "shalom". God's action in history is thus not primarily related to the church but to the world. The church exists for the sake of the world. The church lives "in order that the world may know its true being". The church is that part of humanity which acknowledges and confesses God as the author of historical change. She thus knows and witnesses to the goal of history which God has determined.

The study gave rise to lively debate, but this is not the place to examine that in detail, nor the results of its practical recommendations. However, as we look back at the observations made so far, it becomes clear that any attempt at a theology of history bears the clear stamp of a particular view of the goal of history. Among the basic convictions which underlay and characterized the paradigm was the belief that Christian universalism must have Jesus Christ as its centre and goal. The more universal the theologies of history became, the more formal and faint also became this reference to the Christological centre. Is the tension between the particularity of the Christ event and this universal orientation one that cannot be overcome? This relationship between Christocentrism and universalism was the central issue in a wide-ranging WCC study programme between the New Delhi and Uppsala assemblies with the title "The Finality of Jesus Christ in the Age of Universal History". The Faith and Order study on "God in Nature and History", previously referred to, was an important part of this comprehensive project.

Before we take a final look at this study, we should hear, however, once again the voice of Visser 't Hooft, who constantly remained the leading advocate of Christocentrism. A few years before his retirement as general secretary he published a series of addresses with the title *No Other Name*.[40] At the centre of his reflections lies an analysis of syncretism. He is convinced that syncretistic tendencies in a shrinking pluralistic world represent a greater danger to Christianity than modern atheism. He sees an inclination to syncretism in the strict sense wherever the possibility of a final revelation is in principle denied. This is, however, the indispensable centre of the Christian message: "that God is in Christ and that the deeds of God in Christ are the crucial turning point in the destiny of man".[41] Christianity cannot thus simply class itself as one among the rich variety of the world's religions, but rather views itself "as the adequate and definitive revelation of God in history".[42]

This historically unique Christ event has universal significance in that the "One" has borne the sins of the "many" and saved them by his death (Rom. 5:12ff.). This universality becomes visible in the church as the fellowship of those who respond to God's call to be reconciled, but it passes beyond itself to "the universalism yet to be realized which will find its fulfilment in 'the reconciliation of the world' (Rom. 11:15)". [43]

> Uniqueness, unity [of the church] and universality are all indispensable and mutually interdependent. There is no universality if there is no unique event. But the unique event is not realized in its significance, where there is no movement forward and outward towards universality. And the link between the two is in the body which in its unity, transcending all divisions, is the first fruit of the new humanity. [44]

Visser 't Hooft thus speaks of a "concrete universalism", which represents the true knowledge

> that humanity by itself cannot realize its desire for true universality. Only when it accepts the cross of Christ as the centre of its life the way is opened for the overcoming of the forces that divide men from each other. [45]

In those words the basic theme is sounded once again and in them, too, an internal critical yardstick formulated against the trend to a general theology of history. The concrete centre of universal human history remains the cross of Christ. This theme was also taken up by Hendrikus Berkhof in his address to the Uppsala assembly on "The Finality of Jesus Christ". [46] In his speech he summarizes the insights from the comprehensive study programme of the WCC in the years since New Delhi. He too deals first with objections to the claimed finality of Jesus Christ. He sees it as having its foundation in the resurrection of Jesus Christ from the dead. When the risen Christ is acknowledged "to be the perspective centre of reality", a new vision of the world as a whole opens up. The inclusiveness of the Christ event has been rediscovered in its contemporary reality in the major ecumenical theologies of history.

> However, this tendency is not without serious dangers. If we were to bear in mind only the inclusiveness of Jesus Christ as revealed in his resurrection, we would turn our Christian faith, before being aware of it, into an all-embracing world-view, an ideology beneath which Jesus Christ would change from being the living Lord to become a universal Christocentric principle. [47]

Berkhof names three decisive limitations, or qualifications, to guard us against the temptation to "an ideological triumphalism": the cross, the Spirit, and the future. The cross represents the cost of the new humanity in Christ; the Spirit the fact that it is not at our disposal; and the future the goal of history which is yet to be achieved.

## 6. Summary

It is indisputable that the paradigm of Christocentric universalism gave ecumenical thinking and action after the crisis at the end of the second world war a fresh, clear sense of direction. It has enabled a creative examination to take place of the historical experiences of the end of the "Christian world", advancing secularization, and rapid social change. It has given the ecumenical movement a theological understanding of ecumenism as involving "the whole inhabited earth", and so prepared it to be actively involved in the emergence of a "planetary world". Above all, the paradigm has provided the search for the unity of the church with its distinctive reference point, which transcends all differences and divisions.

This review of some typical moments in the debate has made clear the fascination exerted by this framework of thought. After the static traditional concepts of a "Christian order" and the differences between church and world, of Christian civilization as opposed to non-Christian cultures, of salvation history as opposed to secular history, this dynamic version of an ecumenical theology of history felt like a liberation. It is thus not surprising that Latin American liberation theology in its initial stages clearly drew inspiration from the theme of "sharing in God's action for change in history", which had played such a decisive role in ecumenical debate during those years.

We concluded our review with the address by Berkhof. That cut-off point is arbitrary, as are also the examples selected. The Uppsala assembly with its theme of renewal was, together with the momentum it generated, a superb demonstration of the dynamic power of the paradigm. It was thus not coincidental that the "unity of humankind" became the unofficial theme of that assembly. And the study programme of the Commission on Faith and Order on "The Unity of the Church and the Unity of Humankind" following that assembly was in fact in its initial stages a consistent continuation of the paradigm. Its later development did, admittedly, also reveal the limitations of this framework of thought. We shall return to that later.

In summing up the effects of the paradigm, it should not be overlooked how significant Christocentric universalism has been for the entry of the Orthodox churches into the WCC and for forging links with the Roman Catholic Church. In that theological traditions from the ancient church were rediscovered and expressed in the concepts of Christocentric universalism, Orthodox theologians were in a position to enter into ecumenical debate using their own language. Notable examples of this are the major speeches by Nikos Nissiotis at New Delhi and Metropolitan Ignatios Hazim at Uppsala.

Many references have already been made to the role of the paradigm in forging links with the Roman Catholic Church. Müller-Fahrenholz has examined the similarities and differences of emphasis between ecumenical debate and the documents of the Second Vatican Council. It is in any case clearly apparent that the salvation history approach and Christocentric orientation of major parts of the Constitution on the Church and the Decree on Ecumenism, as well as the dynamic comprehensive understanding of history in the Pastoral Constitution, prepared the way for the subsequent common statement that the World Council of Churches and the Roman Catholic Church are part of "the one ecumenical movement". The opening of the Roman Catholic Church at the Second Vatican Council to the ecumenical movement and the world had been prepared by the work of theologians such as Yves Congar, Karl Rahner and Pierre Teilhard de Chardin. The meeting with similar developments within the ecumenical movement produced a "kairos" which created a new and unexpected ecumenical impetus.

After all has been said, however, we must once again recall the qualifications which became apparent in the contributions by Visser 't Hooft and Berkhof. They are given here as examples of the critical questioning to which the paradigm has been subjected in the whole course of its development. This questioning has been directed at an uncritical dogmatic Christology with its tendency to abstract generalized statements and to docetic triumphalism, which no longer sees the suffering and crucified One in the risen and exalted lord of the church and the world. It has warned of the dangers of turning an ecumenical theology of history into an ideology which plays down the ambiguity of historical processes and the reality of guilt and tragedy, disappointment and death. And it has also registered doubts concerning the tendency to make exaggerated claims for the church and its place in the divine plan of salvation. A salvation history interpretation of the unity of the church in its relationship to the reconciliation of the world as a whole, which does not take seriously the "schism" between the church and Israel, is blind to the fact that the achievement of unity remains hidden in God.[48]

And yet, despite those objections and justified criticisms, it was this framework of thought which sustained the extraordinary missionary consciousness of the ecumenical movement during those years. Here the contrast between the ecumenical movement and the resigned scepticism and militant dogmatic attitudes of our time becomes strikingly clear.

# 3. The New Challenges Facing the Ecumenical Movement

Following that examination of the basic elements of the paradigm and their significance for ecumenical theological work, the suggestion might be made that the thing to do is to make a critical analysis of that position. I shall not do that, but shall return instead to my thesis that a paradigm shift lies before us, or is already happening. Can this hypothesis be verified? A paradigm reaches crisis point when its power to give direction fails before new, unforeseen challenges, when the criteria for identifying problems clearly and the accepted rules for solving them no longer function. The phrase "crisis in the ecumenical movement" appeared soon after the Uppsala assembly and the succeeding years have been marked by increasing tensions.

It would be possible here to follow developments in ecumenical debate since Uppsala and in them to identify the points at which the crisis manifested itself. This would enable us to trace the course of the conflicts which made clear the limits to the ability of the old paradigm to provide orientation. Instead, the analysis which follows begins from the basic elements of the existing paradigm identified in the previous chapter and confronts them with the new challenges in which a changed perception of the overall situation is emerging. In doing so, I shall only partially engage in a systematic reconstruction of the past, since in every case a characteristic debate within the ecumenical movement forms the background.

## 1. Christocentrism and religious pluralism

The expansion of the ecumenical perspective universally to all humanity symbolized by the Uppsala assembly could not ignore the question of the place of religions within the one humanity. It was thus logical that after lengthy preparatory work the WCC initiated in 1971 a programme for Dialogue with People of Other Faiths. The Roman Catholic Church had already, in 1964, set up a secretariat for relations with "non-Christian religions". The significance of this step for the ecumenical movement was emphasized by the fact that at the Nairobi assembly in 1975 a whole section was devoted to the theme "Seeking Community: The Common Search of People of Various Faiths, Cultures and Ideologies".

It was not surprising that, when the report of that section was presented to the assembly plenary, there was open conflict on the theological meaning of dialogue and its relation to the church's missionary task.[1] The "Guidelines on Dialogue", approved by the WCC central committee in 1979, seemed to provide a firm theological basis, but a few years later, at the Vancouver assembly in 1983, controversy broke out afresh.[2]

What was at issue in this passionately conducted debate? Behind the question of the relation of mission to dialogue and the repeatedly expressed concern over "syncretism", i.e. the suspected attempt to create a "universal religion", there lay ultimately the conviction that the ecumenical movement should not under any circumstances abandon its basic Christocentric position. Dialogue with people of other faiths, however desirable it might be on purely human grounds in the interest of peaceful coexistence in society of people with differing religious beliefs, must always remain subordinate to belief in the finality of Jesus Christ and the consequent missionary obligation to proclaim the gospel to all.

The paradigm of "Christocentric universalism" certainly represented a conscious break with the ancient concept of Christendom. Neither Christendom, nor Christian civilization, nor the church had any inherent universal significance. At the centre of God's plan of salvation for the world was his self-revelation in Jesus Christ, who as the eternal Son of God became human for our salvation. In him God had reconciled the world to himself. God had enthroned him as lord of history, indeed of the whole cosmos. Hence, the salvation of the world lay in him alone. Again and again, in the relevant texts referred to in the previous chapter, the emphasis is on the exclusive statements in the New Testament which affirm the exclusive nature of the unsurpassable uniqueness of the way of salvation opened up in Jesus Christ (cf. 1 Cor. 3:11; Acts 4:12; John 14:6; Heb. 10:9ff.; 1 Tim. 2:3ff.). *No Other Name* was the title given by Visser 't Hooft to his programmatic argument against syncretism, both old and new, which he combined with a concise summary of the ecumenical paradigm.

Our historical examination of the origins of the paradigm has made clear that it did not initially arise out of a necessity to define the Christian faith over against other religions. The Christological emphasis had proved necessary in the conflict with liberal cultural Protestantism, and it had received its sharpest expression in its opposition to the claims of totalitarian ideologies. It did, however, quickly become apparent that the exclusive adherence to the revelation of God in Jesus Christ also affected relations with "non-Christian" religions.

The ecumenical debate on this fundamental missiological issue since the meeting of the International Missionary Council in 1938 at Tambaram has often been described.[3] It has long been characterized by the distinction in principle (fully developed in the Barthian theological tradition) between God's self-revelation in Jesus Christ and all human religions, including the religious manifestations of Christianity. In the light of this radical dialectic, all religion is an expression of human self-justification before God, which incurs divine judgment. Karl Barth did in fact move away from that dogmatic position, and the ecumenical movement, following the "biblical realism" of Hendrik Kraemer, had been concerned to reach a deeper understanding of other religions. But the express warning against syncretism by Visser 't Hooft, in the sense of a relativizing of the basic Christocentric orientation, and the predominantly instrumental understanding of dialogue with people of other faiths which we see in Lesslie Newbigin, demonstrate clearly the limits of the ecumenical paradigm with regard to other faiths.[4]

The question of the place of "non-Christian" religions in God's work of salvation in the world could, however, no longer be suppressed by means of prior dogmatic judgments, the clearer it became that the spread of Western civilization to all parts of the world was in no way leading — as Arend van Leeuwen had expected — to the slow extinction of the ancient pre-Christian religions, especially in Asia. Rather, the recovery by those countries of their cultural independence after the end of colonial rule was accompanied by a revival of religious traditions, which often became a symbol of cultural identity. Thus, not only Islam, but also Hinduism and Buddhism displayed new vitality, even as far as making missionary inroads into Western, historically Christian countries.

In contrast to the "exclusive" nature of ecumenical Christocentrism, the "inclusive" position, particularly as it had developed in Roman Catholic theology, appeared to offer ways to a new relationship between Christians and people of other faiths. This position, which is particularly associated with the names of Karl Rahner and Raymond Pannikar, takes up the cosmic, universal-historical significance of the Christ event. It incorporates central themes from the theology of the ancient church. God's will to save, revealed in Christ, applies to all humankind and is at work everywhere, even in the "non-Christian" religions. There is, indeed, no salvation without encounter with Christ; but, wherever people have an experience of grace and salvation in their religions, they are encountering the "hidden Christ" and his work, even though they are not aware of it. They can thus be described as "anonymous Christians", and the church is the "fulfilment" of the yearning for salvation which is alive in the religions of humankind. This "inclusive" version of Christocentrism, which also finds expression in the documents of the Second Vatican Council, is, however, for all its openness to encounter and dialogue with people of other faiths, no less an expression of a dogmatic judgment, the truth of which is presupposed independently of any actual encounter. Other religions are incorporated into the perspective of a Christian universalism, which dialogue can only confirm.[5]

But is it possible, in the present situation of religious pluralism, to hold fast to a dogmatic judgment on the place of other faiths in God's saving action for the world as a conclusion drawn internally from an exclusive or an inclusive basic Christocentric position? We can see in that question the central issue of the contemporary challenge. The phrase "religious pluralism" epitomizes the changed perception of reality. What is meant by it?

Three levels of meaning can be distinguished. *First*, "religious pluralism" describes a situation, occurring in more and more countries, where different religious communities live alongside one another in the same society and need to find ways to live and work together instead of polemical demarcation. *Secondly*, "religious pluralism" denotes the results of a variety of research in the religious field, which, independently of all dogmatic presuppositions, has developed a dynamic and holistic understanding of religion. Religions cannot be reduced to a static system of concepts and beliefs: they are a living whole, which can ultimately only be understood from the inside, and of which personal spirituality, ritual and life-style are an inseparable part. All major religions have changed in many ways, in part through direct influence on one another. *Thirdly*, the phrase "religious pluralism" expresses the experience, arising from numerous interfaith encounters, that opposing truth claims cannot be judged at the level of abstract conceptual analysis, but that they rest on concrete acts of religious commitment, the credibility and authenticity of which can only be disclosed in genuine dialogue.

This awareness of religious pluralism is a development of the last twenty years. First in Asia, and then increasingly throughout the world, it has led to initiatives for dialogue between adherents of different religions, which is characterized by mutual respect and readiness to be enriched and challenged. The more widespread the practice of dialogue becomes — not

between religious systems, but between persons in human community —
the more contentious its theological foundation becomes — and not only
on the Christian side! What is at issue here is the theological interpretation
of religious pluralism. The debate centres on traditional dogmatic Christology, which has also determined the shape of the ecumenical paradigm.

Ecumenical Christocentrism saw itself as a response to the clear
biblical witness to the incarnation and God's reconciling act, and also as
reaffirming the confessions of faith of the ancient church. This classic
position was, however, in the main shaken when the methods of modern
critical research made their way into ecumenical theological work and
made it clear that there was a variety of Christological approaches in the
New Testament. That posed the hermeneutical question as to which
interpretation to adopt. Where, from among the variety of its expressions,
do we find the yardstick for the unity of the New Testament witness to
Christ? How are we to determine the relation between the messianic
language of the original tradition surrounding Jesus in the synoptic
gospels and the incipient incarnation theology in Paul and John? What is
involved when incarnation talk is transferred from its setting of doxologi-
cal language in early Christian hymns or confessions into a context of
conceptual doctrinal statements with universal truth claims?

These questions have in recent years been the object of lively theological debate in connection with efforts to achieve a theological understanding of religious pluralism. In it the Christocentrism of the ecumenical
paradigm has in particular been subjected to critical scrutiny.[6] Although
theological debate is still far from reaching a common answer to this new
challenge, some areas of emphasis on which discussion is being concentrated can none the less be identified.

1. First, there should be mentioned the effort being made to see the
New Testament witness to Christ as embedded in the overall *theocentric*
perspective of the Bible. Biblical universalism is in the first place
theocentric. Belief in the uniqueness of God is valid not for Israel alone
but embraces all peoples. By creation and the covenant with Noah they
are all included in God's work of salvation. At the end of time God will
gather the nations together from all the corners of the earth and establish
God's rule. This theocentric orientation, which is a feature of the
preaching and practice of Jesus himself, must be given fresh emphasis
today to counter a deeply rooted "Christomonism" which

> tends to regard Jesus Christ as "the Christians' God" and makes it impossible
> to have any meaningful dialogue with neighbours of other faiths.[7]

This means, theologically, to take Trinitarian belief seriously, and above all to incorporate the work of the Holy Spirit into our understanding of the Christ event.

2. From that there further follows the effort to achieve a *concrete Christology*, which takes seriously the historical particularity of Jesus. Belief in the incarnation should not become a metaphysical principle, but must remain related to the concrete, unique human being Jesus of Nazareth, who lived as a Jew, and who paid for his life of total devotion to God his Father and to the least of his people by his death on the cross. Instead of a Christology "from above", which is above all oriented towards belief in the divinity of Jesus Christ as the second person of the Trinity, a Christology "from below" must come to the fore, acknowledging and confessing in the human being Jesus God's loving and liberating care for all, particularly those far from God.

3. Finally, as well as the cosmic, universal, historical perspective, it must also be our concern to recover the *messianic orientation* which looks forward to God's universal rule. Belief in Christ's present rule over church and world must not blind us to the fact that even his rule is directed to the future, when God will be "all in all" (1 Cor. 15:28). It was Berkhof who referred to this not yet achieved goal of God's historical dealings with the world as a "qualification" warning us against "ideological triumphalism". This orientation to God's universal rule as the goal of human history is particularly important to prevent Christ-centred belief from surreptitiously becoming church-centred belief. God's universal rule is closely linked in the New Testament with the gift of the Spirit as the "pledge" or "foretaste" of the End. The action of God's Spirit cannot, however, be confined to institutions. The Spirit "blows where the Spirit wills" (John 3:8). The Orthodox tradition particularly has constantly made reference to the importance of the theology of the Holy Spirit for relations with other faiths.[8]

## 2. Christian universalism and the logic of the "global system"

The universal thrust of the ecumenical paradigm found succinct expression in the conviction of the Uppsala assembly that the "unity of humankind" is a central element in the ecumenical calling of the churches. With the spread of modern science and technology and the development of world structures of trade and communication, all parts of the world were increasingly growing together into an interwoven whole. This fact seemed in the light of God's plan of salvation for humankind to be a sharp challenge to the still divided churches in the ecumenical movement.

The WCC Commission on Faith and Order thus initiated soon after the Uppsala assembly a study programme on the theme "The Unity of the Church and the Unity of Humankind".[9] Very quickly, however, critical voices were raised questioning the universalist perspective of its approach: the study viewed humankind as a dynamic "community of shared becoming", and, like the previous study on "God in nature and history", ignored the historical realities of suffering, evil and tragedy.[10] In face of the manifest conflicts and tensions in the human community was it possible to speak of the unity of humankind in any other way but as a future hope? The Commission on Faith and Order, meeting in Louvain in 1971, thus placed the ecumenical quest for the unity of the church in the more realistic context of the typical areas of tension in human life: the new awareness of the variety of cultures, the struggle for worldwide social and economic justice, the struggle against racism, the new experience of religious pluralism, and the marginalization of the handicapped in church and society. That list contains almost all the challenges in which in the period following the Uppsala assembly the limitations of ecumenical universalism became apparent — the exception being the issue of the community of women and men in church and society, which became a main focus of work in its own right in a later phase of the study.

The convoluted and controversial progress of this Faith and Order study can be interpreted in many respects as early evidence of an impending paradigm shift. At least, the interim report produced by the Commission at its meeting in Accra in 1974 represents a considerable modification of the initial universalist perspective. It clearly names the dangers and drawbacks of increasing worldwide interdependence.

> In the name of unity and interdependence, false structures are created...
> Hence it may be more accurate to speak of human brokenness than of
> mankind's unity.[11]

Later in this brief statement there appear the key words "liberation", "conflict" and "solidarity", revealing that a change in perspective has already taken place.

The decisive symbolic break with the universalist paradigm came with the initiation in 1969 of the Programme to Combat Racism. It arose out of the painful realization that traditional liberal hopes for inter-racial equality and reconciliation in one integrated society had collapsed in the face of the reality of structural racism. Racial conflict, particularly in Southern Africa, was no longer a "problem", which could be solved by traditional political measures, no longer a "crisis" within the existing order, which could be overcome. It had become a struggle by the oppressed and those with no rights for liberation from unjust power structures, a struggle whose goal was "redistribution of power". With that key phrase the fundamental conflict was sparked off. [12]

What has here been compressed into one section by way of example, i.e. domination and dependency as structural counterparts, came increasingly to the fore in subsequent years as the core of the North-South conflict between rich and poor. It was thus impossible to remain neutral, and the ecumenical movement had to choose between interpreting these worldwide developments either "from above", i.e. from the perspective of domination, of those in power, or "from below", i.e. from the perspective of dependency, of the victims. Thus, when the world mission conference in Bangkok in 1972 interpreted the universal "Salvation Today" in terms of the liberation struggles, open conflict broke out in the ecumenical movement, for this in fact represented a basic challenge to the universalist paradigm.

The challenge became yet sharper as a consequence of a series of external crises and factors affecting ecumenical debate. These included: perception of the failure of current development efforts directed towards modernization, growth and economic integration — dramatically symbolized by the famines in the Sahel region and in Ethiopia in 1972-74; the increasing militarization of political life and the cynical disregard of fundamental human rights for the sake of so-called "national security"; and the disturbing awareness of the "limits to growth" produced by the Club of Rome's study published in 1972 and reinforced by the effects of the so-called oil crisis of 1973. Finally, they also included the experience of victory and defeat in the struggles of popular movements against foreign and domestic oppression in Chile, Vietnam, Iran and Zimbabwe.

What has here only been alluded to briefly formed the concrete background for the changed perception which found expression in the key phrase "world crisis", which cropped up in all discussions during these years. The meeting of the WCC central committee in Berlin in 1974 marked the actual turning point in the post-Uppsala development in regard to ecumenical universalism. There the central committee received with great dismay reports on "Threats to Survival", on "The Economic Threat to Peace", and on the Bucharest conference on "Science and Technology for Human Development". [13] This conference particularly had by use of the new key word "sustainability" identified the challenge that consideration of the future of humankind and particularly of the effects of science and technology should be related to the wider context of the future of creation. Thus human-centred universalism was critically outstripped and expanded on the one hand and at the same time revealed as seriously endangered by its own actions. What was for some a "world crisis" for which solutions had to be found, was for others — and that means for the majority of humankind — increasingly a struggle for mere survival. The tension between these two perceptions runs through all subsequent debate. It is also an important clue to understanding the alienation between the WCC and the Roman Catholic Church, which began at that time, for, apart from anything else, the Vatican held determinedly firm to the universalist perspective, as is shown by the arguments over Latin American liberation theology, which began during those years.

The WCC has responded to this challenge, presented on the one hand by the escalating North-South conflict and on the other by the impending environmental crisis, by attempting to formulate the basic elements of a new paradigm, a vision of a goal for ecumenical work in the changed world situation. The intensive debate in the years 1976-79 on a "just, participatory and sustainable society" arose out of the change of perspective which had meanwhile taken place: from "development" to "liberation"; from "modernization and economic growth" to the defence of "the right to life" for all, including the world of non-human life and the life of future generations; from "overcoming crises" to "struggle against unjust structures"; from dialogue with experts and appeal to those in positions of responsibility to the promotion of the independence and empowerment of the marginalized majority of humankind.

Theologically, these debates marked the transition from the classic perspective of "the kingship of Christ" over the church and the world to God's kingdom seen in messianic perspective, which takes its bearings from Jesus of Nazareth, who in his solidarity with the poor and the marginalized and in his powerlessness on the cross, was acknowledged as the hidden Messiah, the embodiment of the promised kingdom of God. But precisely this change of perspective, from "above" to "below", provoked opposition, and not only in the WCC central committee, when the results of this debate were presented in Jamaica in 1979.[14] Despite the objections clearly expressed by defenders of the old paradigm, the new approach continued to exert influence. It is particularly remarkable that it was acknowleged and developed in the course of the ecumenical efforts beginning at the end of the 1970s to formulate a new ethical and political frame of reference for understanding paradigmatically the significance of the world economic crisis.[15]

The change of perspective resulted in the ambiguity of political, economic and cultural interdependence being perceived yet more sharply. Behind the processes which had led to this close interweaving of human-kind, there could now be discerned a deliberate project of the "oikoumene", or world order, which was directed towards expanding the market model worldwide to all areas of life and which was being driven forward particularly by the great transnational corporations. The internationalization of production, trade and finance is a development which has taken place at great speed since the first recession in the world economy as a consequence of the so-called oil crisis. It represents a truly radical change in the world economy, and has led to a conclusive hardening of dependency structures. For the first time it is now possible to speak of a closed world system, which follows its own rationality and logic, independently of human needs, and either rejects the goals of justice, participation and sustainability as illusory and irrational, or else recognizes them only to the extent that they do not disturb the balance which the system demands.

Closer analysis of this process of "transnationalization" and its effects on the living conditions of the majority of people in the poor dependent nations led in the course of an ecumenical study to the conclusion that this transnational "oikoumene" must inevitably come into conflict with the basic beliefs of the ecumenical movement. The logic of a movement whose goal is human community in solidarity is opposed to the logic of such a closed global system.

> The transnational corporations cannot be converted to ecumenism. Their economicist, exclusive and hierarchical logic makes this impossible. The ecumenical movement cannot compromise its commitment to a holistic, human-centred approach to development and its prime commitment to the poor. [16]

This analysis was later developed further by José Míguez Bonino at an ecumenical symposium in honour of Philip Potter. In the light of the debt crisis as a consequence of the international finance system he speaks of the "oikoumene of domination", which is the opposite of the "oikoumene of solidarity". He continues:

> The system of ecumenical domination and the movement of ecumenical solidarity do not represent symmetrical realities. In the first case we have an established *system* which occupies the oikoumene, determines the structural relations within it, assigns roles and resources, sets the laws, regulates communications and establishes the mechanisms of control and of the repro-

duction of the system. It operates with a rationality it has developed and which prescribes the limits of reality, proscribing as irrational and unreal whatever does not correspond to its "reason". I would like to suggest that this systemic rationality pervades the whole life of the oikoumene, from the economic world of the multinationals to the political organizations, the defence systems, the world extension of mass media, and the cultural and religious world bodies, including the WCC...

I would also claim that this system and its rationality are inherently oppressive, predicated on a logic of domination and leading to dehumanization. At the WCC assembly in Vancouver it was characterized as "a system of death" which cannot incorporate the idea of real change and transformation because it is built on a principle of absolute immanence, in fact, on an absolutely closed materialism within which the qualitatively "new", and consequently real, transcendence cannot be seen except as absurd and irrational. Within it change can only be understood as quantitative and the human as subordinate to the technical. Conversion is impossible — except for a miracle. And the miracle definitely has to explode the rationality of the system. This is the tragic — in the original Greek sense of tragedy — predicament of the system.

On the other hand, we have the movement of solidarity which rests on a qualitatively different logic and rationality: the presence of transcendence, the search for the immanence of the new future latent in reality and, therefore, the search for a praxis which releases this future. This is the rationality of faith, for which the reality of God is more decisive than the reality of the world as it is. Its logic reinforces life and the human and demands a constant *anakainosis tou noos*, the transformation of understanding, repentance and conversion. [17]

I have quoted Míguez Bonino's analysis of the two visions of the oikoumene at such length because it provides a succinct summary of the situation of transition. Universalism, which includes the meaning of the Greek word "oikoumene", i.e. the whole inhabited earth, has been taken down from its idealistic pedestal and related to the concrete reality of the closed "global system". One aspect of the New Testament understanding of "oikoumene", i.e. the threatening power structures of the Roman empire, is thus being taken seriously again after having been completely thrust into the background by the ecumenical movement in its fascination with universalism. But, if the only attitude which the ecumenical movement can take up against this system is that of a decisive "no" to the "spirit, logic and practice" [18] of the "oikoumene of domination", then it would seem that the total negation of universalism has been reached. Is there no solution to this impasse? Indeed, in face of the manifest superior power of the "oikoumene of domination" and the lack of success of many ecumenical efforts at solidarity, must we not accept that the "oikoumene of solidarity" is at best utopian, or at worst nothing more than an illusion?

That is to state the dilemma, for which no solution is yet in sight. But perhaps the first step to be taken consists in accepting that there is no such thing as *the* solution. Problems can be solved within an established frame of reference of rules, criteria and goals. The acute problems of this period of transition do not lend themselves to a "solution". Instead they require a readiness to endure, be patient and in many cases to suffer. If this is correct, then careful critical self-examination is necessary in face of the tendency to respond to the absolute claim of the global system to power and control with an absolute refusal, or indeed "demonization", of its structures or their representatives. Prophetic denial can be necessary as a result of concrete analysis, as for example in the case of racism, but even in such a denial there can be a latent submission to the absolute claims of the system. Indeed, the task consists rather in achieving liberation from obsession with global realities, in unmasking and demythologizing the philosophy of the global system as a dangerous illusion, and in discovering the logic of life, i.e. the reality of relationships, a logic in accord with the practice of sharing and solidarity. It points away from the oikoumene as global system to the oikoumene of the house of life, of the habitable earth, which, if it is to remain habitable, will involve concrete human stewardship in solidarity. In this turning away from the deadly illusion of the global system and turning towards the messianic vision of "God dwelling with humankind" (Rev. 21:3), we see the outline of a new paradigm beyond Christian universalism taking shape.[19]

## 3. Salvation history and the threat to survival

The ecumenical theology of history developed as a response to a deeper interpretation of secularization, which was understood as a consequence of radical historical change. Secularization meant the collapse of traditional orders and structures, whether they existed by the law of nature or by God's creative will, whether they were metaphysically or politically legitimated. Van Leeuwen had included all these in the concept of "ontocracy" and saw secularization as the final overthrow of ontocracy by "theocracy". In place of an ordered cosmos there now appears the world of history, in which God's action is accomplished. Thus secularization means the complete historicization of human existence. This all-embracing social change is not a break with or rebellion against a divine order: it can now rather be itself understood as the effect of God's action to bring about change. God himself is acknowledged as the author of historical change. Through the incarnation God has hallowed history and by means of change God is leading history towards its goal — the establishment of the divine shalom. Where this dynamic understanding of history was associated with the history of nature in the processes of evolution, the result was a "naturalization" of salvation history, an identification of God's action with the evolutionary dynamism of the world of history. With hindsight it is evident that this theology of history could perhaps only have arisen in the context of experience of far-reaching changes, particularly in Europe and North America after the second world war, and that it was there that it was most widely accepted.

The *first* protest against this view of a universal salvation history was expressed as early as 1966 at the Geneva conference on Church and Society from a Latin American standpoint, and was in the following years discussed under the easily misunderstood key phrase "theology of revolution". Richard Shaull and others at that time confronted the view of history as determined by an evolutionary philosophy of development with a dialectical view of history based on social conflict: history is not simply "development", but is constantly a place of struggle for justice and power, for liberation from oppressive orders and structures. God's action in history is thus experienced not in the evolutionary processes of change but in the revolutionary breakthrough of something new. The exodus, the liberation of Israel from the house of bondage in Egypt, becomes the basic symbol of God's action in history. What we see here is no longer a positive interpretation of the changes to which we are doomed as something in which we can "participate". Our response to God's action in history must consist in actively helping forward the processes of liberation and of revolutionary change.

Initially, by means of this "prophetic" interpretation of history, only the basic approach of salvation history was radicalized and at the same time the eschatological nature of the absolutely new in God's action was contrasted with the tendency to "naturalize" salvation history. Here too, the contextuality of this thinking, which was related to the political and social situation in Latin America in the 1960s, can be clearly seen.

The tension between these two historical perspectives continued for a time beyond the Uppsala assembly. But it subsequently became increasingly clear that the view that history as a whole was the work of God must collapse. The history of those in power did not run its course in parallel, either in time or direction, with the history of the dependent and oppressed. The white history of progress came into conflict with the black history of liberation. The question as to how God's action is to be discerned and which side of history God is on, became an open matter of contention in ecumenical debate.

"History" thus came up against its limits as the decisive linchpin in the paradigm of Christian universalism. The unity of history can in any case only be conceived and expressed as a proleptic or eschatological unity: history possesses unity only in the light of its end. This unity remains rooted in God's action, and the symbol of the kingdom of God took on fresh significance in ecumenical debate, after having been thrust completely into the background in the preceding decades. Before its completion, which is hidden in God, history, however, remains ambiguous, characterized by contradictions, conflicts and crises. Constant reference is now made to the fact that Israel itself did not go straight from the exodus from Egypt into the Promised Land. Between the two lay the wanderings, conflicts and temptations in the wilderness. [20] Indeed, God's self-revelation in history in Jesus Christ led to the crisis of the cross: there is no intra-historical continuity from the cross to God's new act in raising Jesus Christ from the dead by the power of God's life-giving Spirit.

The *second* objection to the theology of history paradigm has to do with the emergence of environmental awareness at the beginning of the 1970s. The publication of the study by the Club of Rome came as a shock, for unlimited growth had become the symbolic foundation of the modern history of progress. Since then a far-reaching change of consciousness has taken place and the pressing problems of the environment have become a priority political issue the world over. We know today that the historicization of nature, i.e. its domestication by humankind by means of science, technology and industry, is an attack on the future prospects of historical life. The long-term consequences of growth-oriented production and the over-exploitation of non-renewable natural resources threaten the survival of the human race and our natural environment.

This new awareness has become yet more clearly defined in face of the dangers arising from the military and civilian use of nuclear energy. The threat of a possible nuclear holocaust, which would destroy all life on earth, alters basically our historical perspective, which reckons on an open future. Equally decisive is the growing recognition that the civilian use of nuclear energy involves incalculable risks for an unforeseeable future.

The "growth society" of the decades since the second world war has visibly become a "risk society", which must constantly devote increasing effort and expenditure to avoiding possible lethal mistakes. But, if human beings as subjects of history have to function perfectly and free from error, so as to avoid destroying themselves, then it is no longer human history in the traditional sense. History has now become a closed system, whose most important goal is self-preservation. In such a history controlled by the system, there is no longer any place for divine action, nor for responsible human action, for responsibility presupposes people who can accept liability for errors, mistakes and wrongdoing.

The foregoing paragraph has followed lines which admittedly have not yet found any clearly discernible echo in ecumenical debate. The reason for that lies above all in the still unresolved differences of approach: the new commitment to the "integrity of creation" stands over against the continuing obligation to struggle for "justice". That once again epitomizes the situation of transition. How is this tension to be understood? Is the opposition between sustainability and justice as criteria for ecumenical action, which was to the fore at the time of the great world conference on "Faith, Science and the Future" in Cambridge, USA, in 1979, simply a reflection of the North-South conflict which we examined in the preceding section?[21] Is there behind the environmental commitment and the ecological movements of the industrialized nations a latent evasion of the demands for social and economic justice throughout the world? The fact that the same tension, with minor variations of emphasis, is at present also evident in debates within feminist theology must reduce our hope that these contradictory approaches will be resolved or at least lead to a complementary relationship between the two poles of tension.

However, as in previous sections, an attempt should be made to think beyond the now discernible limitations of the former paradigm. The starting point for this attempt must be the insight that the history of humankind is embedded in the history of nature: it is part of the history of *life*. The reduction of history to human interaction thus proves to be a dangerous — and indeed potentially lethal — abstraction. Historical change, resulting from human action, is built on the permanence of natural cycles and the interaction of all living beings, in which the foundations of life are constantly being regenerated and reproduced. The modern approach to history with its anthropocentric orientation has ignored this vital (i.e. life-giving) foundation of human history, and indeed the history of human action modelled on growth and production with the goal of increasing wealth is progressively destroying the foundations of its own life. It thus shows itself to be a history of violence, which is turning not only against nature but also against the principal means of preserving and reproducing the foundations of human life. Women are the most obvious victims of this history of violence. Only if they become integrated into the processes of work and production do they become subjects of history in their own right. In so doing they are compelled to leave behind their awareness of the wider context of the history of all living beings.

If this is correct, then we must also critically challenge talk of God which is exclusively concerned with God's action as bringing about change and creating something new. Old Testament theology in interpreting the wisdom tradition has in recent years made us aware once again of the biblical witness to God's work of preservation and blessing.[22] God has not left the creation to its own devices. As the source of all life, God, like a mother, constantly cares for the life of all created beings. Jürgen Moltmann has spoken of the sabbath as the "completion of creation".[23] The sabbath is the symbol of creation at rest: it applies to human beings, the beasts and the earth. Human activity inevitably intervenes in the cycles of life, but it must pause, so that the vitality of all created beings can be regularly renewed. God's justice, moreover, is to be seen above all in protecting the possibilities of life of those who are not "subjects of their own history". Righteousness, i.e. communal action for justice, takes concrete form in Israel's Torah in the requirement to "hold back", for the rich and the powerful to refrain from exercising their rights and powers over the poor, widows and orphans. The biblical tradition is realistic in its attitude to the conflictual nature of humankind's history of violence. The ordinances of God's covenant do not have an ideal society as their goal, but the containment of conflicts between human beings and nature and between human beings themselves, by means of periodic redistributions of power, so as to protect the possibilities of life for all created beings. They are above all protective ordinances, which lay down the limits beyond which human history will destroy itself.

The biblical view of *justice* is that its aim is protection, the preservation of the possibilities of life for all living beings, and respect for the "right to life" in face of the effects of a potentially self-destructive system. Such a view does away with the conflict between our duty to work for "justice" and our commitment to the "integrity of creation". That is, of course, only valid if sustainability is viewed as a criterion for preserving the sacred gift of life and not as a criterion for holding in balance incompatible demands within the system. The goal is not the continuance of a closed system of human history but the preservation of the history of all living beings in face of the effects of humankind's history of violence.

There thus opens up a more comprehensive view of history as the inner relationship between all living beings. God, the source of all life, is part of this history, and at the same time stands over against it in freedom. God creates new life out of death and through the crises of humankind's history of violence will bring about the new creation, eternal life in God's presence. The history of human action with its conflicts takes place within the divine *oikonomia*, within the divinely protected household of life. God's action within human history serves to contain violence and is directed towards protecting the lives of its victims. The self-surrender of Jesus Christ to the violence of the cross is the symbol that God will ultimately overcome humankind's history of violence, the enmity between God and humankind, the enmity between human beings, and the enmity between humankind and creation. In Jesus Christ God has placed himself at the point where life's relationships are broken, and so brought about "reconciliation".

The New Testament way of describing God's action in history is to speak of the Spirit of God at work. The Spirit is the gift of the last days, God's eschatological presence in history. The life-giving Spirit of God, who brings things different and opposed to one another together into a new relationship, represents the global history of all living beings within human history. Where God's Spirit is at work, the opposite of humankind's history of violence becomes evident, for the Spirit "will confute the world, and show where wrong and right and judgment lie" (John 16:8).

This approach thus also opens up the inner connection between the messianic symbol of the kingdom, the rule of God, in the synoptic tradition, the Pauline symbol of the body of Christ, which is built and held together by the Spirit of God, and the Johannine symbol of "eternal life", life in its fullness. The perspective of the kingdom, the rule of God, corresponds to the language of prophecy, which speaks of God as casting down the mighty from their thrones and exalting the lowly (Luke 1:52). This prophetic protest against humankind's history of violence is as necessary today as it was in the days of Israel's prophets and of Jesus. The prophetic protest reveals human history in its true colours and thus heightens the crisis. And then the symbols of the body of Christ and of eternal life testify that in the resurrection of Jesus Christ from the dead God has broken the vicious circle of the history of violence and created new life. The eschatological gift of new life through the Spirit of God inaugurates the new creation, the renewed history of all living beings. This "salvation history", the divine *oikonomia*, extends into human history, but is never coterminous with it this side of the End. Where this eschatological tension between salvation history and secular history is removed, then the "naturalization" of salvation history naturally follows on. That results in ecumenical theology losing its ability to engage in prophetic criticism of the concrete history of human action and its self-destructive effects. Only in this critical perspective can we speak justifiably and meaningfully of "salvation history".

## 4. Unity and diversity in the church

Analysis of the current ecumenical paradigm had shown clearly that concentration on the church and its unity was a direct consequence of belief in the universal significance of the Christ event. The visible unity of the church was understood to be the decisive witness to the real union of divine and human reality in the incarnation of God in Jesus Christ and to the universal rule of Jesus Christ over world and church. Indeed, the global unity of the people of God stood in direct relationship in salvation history to the final ingathering of the whole human race under God's rule. The ecclesiological orientation of the paradigm and the debate in the ecumenical movement determined by it is thus not an additional element but rather the central element of the paradigm itself. It has up to now been the distinguishing feature of theological work in the ecumenical field as compared with theological debate in the various churches.

The ecumenical paradigm had already fully developed when the Second Vatican Council placed the issue of the church at the centre of theological attention, and indeed far beyond the domain of the Roman Catholic Church. The Dogmatic Constitution on the Church, *Lumen Gentium*, was the fruit of a fundamental renewal of Roman Catholic ecclesiology. This new direction had been fostered particularly by Roman Catholic theologians in France, Germany and the Netherlands, and displayed many parallels with contemporary theological thought in the ecumenical movement. In the course of unofficial conversations, a mutually fruitful exchange had begun long before the first official approach of the Roman Catholic Church to the ecumenical movement.

Despite its being unmistakably Catholic in tone, the ecclesiology of the Dogmatic Constitution on the Church is in many respects closely related to the ecclesiological positions which had developed in the course of ecumenical debate since 1952. This is to be seen in its biblical, salvation-history approach, its Christocentrism, its fresh appreciation of the independence of local churches and their fellowship in the universal church, and lastly in the belief that all lay people as members of the people of God are called to participate in the threefold ministry of Jesus Christ. The explicit inclusion of the ecclesiology of the ancient church centred on the celebration of the eucharist in the Constitution on the Liturgy fruitfully strengthened dialogue with the Orthodox churches in the ecumenical movement. The possibility of direct entry into WCC membership by the Roman Catholic Church, which was being openly considered at the time of the Uppsala assembly and immediately afterwards, is confirmation of the unifying power of the ecumenical paradigm.

The previous sections have each shown how in a particular area the paradigm in the years following the Uppsala assembly reached its limits as it confronted new challenges. Because of the central role of ecclesiology in the paradigm and its indissoluble connection with the other elements, i.e. Christocentrism, the universal orientation, and history as the central category of interpretation, it is to be expected that the difficulties indicated should also be reflected in ecumenical debate on the church and its unity and that they might well reinforce one another. Thus in fact the problems involved in a Christology "from above" have had a direct effect on the ecclesiology on which it had been a determining influence: it became "triumphalist" in tone and more and more difficult to verify by appeal to actual experience of what the church is. The universalist current in thinking on unity at least tends to inhibit perception of obvious conflicts and differences, not only in secular society but in the church itself. Where from a salvation-history viewpoint history is overexalted and suffused in glory, then also the essentially historical nature of the church is ultimately lost from view.

It is thus not surprising that the new directions I have mentioned, which attempt to go beyond the current ecumenical paradigm, also concentrate on discussions on a future ecumenical ecclesiology. Critical revision of the ecclesiological assumptions and implications of the current paradigm is increasingly seen as one of the decisive tasks to be undertaken in the present situation of transition.

This revision, or further development, has been decisively taken forward in Roman Catholic theology since the Council. In this process, the compromise nature of the ecclesiological statements in the Constitution on the Church has become clearly evident. The tensions not resolved at the time of the Council have led to open conflicts in the process of ecclesiastical and theological reception and have made the initial assumption that the basic ecclesiological positions corresponded with the ecumenical movement appear increasingly questionable. Two trends can be distinguished in the reception of the ecclesiology of the Council. On the one hand are the many attempts to move on from Christocentric universalism to a "communio" ecclesiology based on the Trinity, which makes it possible to take seriously in a new way the historical nature of the church as a community of disciples and as a prophetic sign of the kingdom of God. By contrast, on the other hand, we see a retreat to the classic pre-Council Catholic position of a universalist ecclesiology, legal and hierarchical in style, with emphasis on unity as uniformity of doctrine and church order. While the first trend is able to participate usefully in ecumenical debate, dialogue with the second trend is becoming increasingly difficult.

In the work of the WCC too, particularly in the Commission on Faith and Order, a critical further development of the ecclesiological assumptions of the former paradigm has taken place. I have already indicated how close is the first position within the debate going on in the Roman Catholic Church. The statement on unity by the New Delhi assembly had already interpreted the goal of unity as "one fully committed fellowship". "Fellowship", in the sense of "communio" or "koinonia", has since then become a key ecclesiological concept. More recently, since the Uppsala assembly, the Christocentric orientation has been expanded and amplified by rooting the ecclesial fellowship in the work of the Holy Spirit. Lastly, talk of the church as a "sign" of the kingdom of God has opened up the possibility of overcoming the above-mentioned tension between a sacramental, ontological ecclesiology and a prophetic, functional ecclesiology. Where the church is understood as a "sign", the eschatological distinction is maintained between the perfect fellowship of the kingdom of God and the empirical reality of the church with its contradictions and inconsistencies.

All these attempts at a further development are, admittedly, still marked by a largely unquestioned agreement on the actually existing image of the church. It has been shaped by the form taken by the church in history as an institutionally constituted corporate body in society. But meanwhile a conspicuous change in the form of the church has been taking place. The question "Who is the church?" is again being seen to be an open question. In Latin America, in the light of the spread of "base communities", there is talk of "ecclesiogenesis", i.e. the birth of a new form of the church.[24] Here the institutional distinctions between church and world and church and society fall into the background. What is important is fellowship which can be concretely experienced and solidarity between the members of a community. The resulting variety of social forms of the church is no longer seen as a problem but as a liberating enrichment, but it does also point up an obvious limitation in the universalist language of traditional ecclesiology.

The decisive challenge to the former paradigm thus lies in the increasingly clear perception that there is a growing and inevitable variety within and between the churches. While this variety in the domain of the Roman Catholic Church, which is a worldwide church, is above all an internal problem to that church, in the wider context of the ecumenical movement it is linked with the emergence of local, context-related forms of church life, which depart from the traditional model of the church. The immense variety of independent churches in Africa and Pentecostal churches in Latin America dramatically illustrates this challenge. The question of the relation between unity and variety, or diversity, in the church has become a test case for the ability of the ecumenical paradigm to provide orientation, since it has been totally directed towards the visible unity of the church.

It is thus not surprising that since the Uppsala assembly the issue of the relation of variety, or diversity, to the unity of the church has moved to the centre of debate. Ecclesiological thought, which had crystallized around the key words "catholicity" and "conciliarity", has been constantly influenced by the problem of variety, and by means of the concept of "reconciled diversity" this variety has been incorporated as a constitutive element into our understanding of the unity of the church. Closer examination has, however, made clear that the problem of diversity arises in very diverse ways, so that it is impossible to make one single judgment. A distinction must be made between the variety of confessional traditions and the variety of cultural and social contexts which lead to different forms of the church. While there are here differences between the churches, various new social forms of the church have come into being within the institutionally unified churches in the form of base communities, action groups and campaigns, movements and communities. Many of these new forms of church life are interconfessional in nature, but the fears that they will give rise to a new confession have so far not been realized. All major churches are, however, experiencing the necessity within their inherited structures of coming to terms with the collapse of their monopoly claim as an institution and of re-establishing and maintaining their own unity in face of this internal variety of social forms.

The problem of unity and diversity in the church is further complicated where differences of sex, class or race threaten the overall fellowship of everyone within the church. The incorporation of apartheid into church structures, discrimination against women in a church dominated by men, marginalization of persons with handicaps, and the virtual exclusion of the lowest social classes from a middle-class church — all these situations radically call in question traditional talk of the visible unity of the church.

In the context of an ecclesiology based on the visible unity of the church as "God's gift and our task", a unity whose foundation is Jesus Christ, it would seem appropriate to seek a solution to the problem by distinguishing between "legitimate" and "illegitimate" diversity. Thus in the course of the study on the theme "The Unity of the Church and the Unity of Humankind", the criterion of "diversity centred on Christ" was considered.[25] Here the danger of idealistic and triumphalist talk of the unity of the church can be seen. In face of the tensions and contradictions in the life of the church such talk becomes at best irrelevant and at worst an instrument of domination to suppress diversity. According to the criterion of "diversity centred on Christ", diversity is not to be regarded as lack of unity. The only access we have to Jesus Christ is to him as crucified, and proclaimed and believed in as the risen One. Witness to Jesus Christ only becomes Good News when it is proclaimed concretely, when it enters ever afresh into human history, culture and life situations. Only in that way does it prove to be truth, power for living and a liberating protest against self-destructive human history. The diversity of creeds, theologies and church orders in the days of the New Testament and the ancient church was not felt to be a denial of unity in Christ. The same diversity is also to be expected today wherever the gospel is concretely proclaimed and expressed in the common life of humankind. While "catholicity" is a description of the inner quality and fullness of this life of the church, which takes many forms but all of them rooted in Jesus Christ, "conciliarity" refers to the efforts made to maintain the discipline of the fellowship in its diversity. The limits of diversity are reached when they lead to division, reciprocal exclusion, or a refusal of fellowship.[26]

Meanwhile, however, there has been a further shift in the debate. The starting point is no longer the unity given us in Christ as "God's gift and our task" which must be made visible and real, but the actually existing differences. The unity of the church must be achieved, restored, preserved or defended in face of opposing positions within the one church. The measure of unity is understanding, consensus in doctrine and church order. If the former paradigm was unashamedly "vertical" in its talk of the unity of the church, now a "horizontal" understanding of unity is gaining ground in the sense of a rapprochement between different traditions and positions. This trend towards a horizontal understanding of unity, which is ultimately a matter of church politics, has been reinforced by the increased internal diversity within the major churches, particularly the Roman Catholic Church. The maintenance of the unity and integrity of one's own church has become the supreme aim of church leaders. Thus, reconciliation, balancing the differences between church traditions, is, it must be realistically admitted, the maximum ecumenical unity which can be achieved.

As a result of this shift in emphasis, talk of the "unity of the church" has become highly questionable. It has, of course, been repeatedly emphasized in ecumenical debate that unity does not mean uniformity, but the application of the concept of unity to church politics and the difficulty inherent in holding unity and diversity together in tension brings again to mind the problematic historical ancestry of unity thinking as an instrument of domination. Again and again in the course of church history dissidents have been excluded or violently persecuted by invoking the "unity of the church". Indeed, it is possible to defend the thesis that most divisions in the history of the church have been the consequence of carrying concern for unity too far. [27] In any case, diversity only becomes a problem if it is measured against a normative scale of unity. The question must thus be asked whether we should not stop using the idea of "the unity of the church" in ecumenical debate because of the easily misunderstood and static, abstract nature of the concept.

The biblical concept of "fellowship" or "communion", in its vertical dimension as participation in the divine reality through Jesus Christ in the Holy Spirit, and in its horizontal dimension as sharing with one another in a life of solidarity, is better suited to give direction to the ecumenical movement. That is, as long as it is clear that with this as our goal we are not thinking of a static situation, which can be expressed conceptually or even institutionally, but of a dynamic process, which will be completed only at the End. The divine fellowship of the Trinity as a relationship between different persons opens up an understanding of fellowship which goes beyond its modern restricted meaning of a fellowship of the like-minded as opposed to "society". Fellowship does not come into being as the result of individuals joining together on the basis of common commitment, belief or inclination. The abiding difference of the other person is rather a condition for the possibility of relationship and fellowship. Independence and relationship have a common origin. Diversity and fellowship reciprocally condition each other. The reality of fellowship can only be experienced in relationship with those who are different — not apart from, prior to, or independently of such a relationship. [28]

The concept of "fellowship", arrived at from a social interpretation of the doctrine of the Trinity, opens up the possibility of progressing beyond the insoluble tension within the former paradigm between unity and diversity. It takes seriously the differences between the churches and within the life of each church, but its chief concern is to identify the constitutive relatedness between those who differ from one another. "Fellowship" is more than a critical principle: its goal is to become visibly real. Thus criteria for this visible fellowship must be identified and elaborated. One indication, which will be taken up again later, can be given here: it is universal Christian belief that baptism, as the act of incorporation into the body of Christ, establishes the basic bond of fellowship between all who confess Jesus Christ. This fellowship is not founded on our confession of faith, nor on the sacramental action of the church. It is rather the Holy Spirit, who, out of the many who are and remain different from one another, causes the one body of Christ to grow. Confession of Jesus Christ and baptism are the visible signs which are antecedent to all our ecumenical efforts to make the fellowship of the church visible.

## 5. Summary

By examining four typical challenges which have emerged in the period following the Uppsala assembly, we have clearly seen the limitations inherent in the former paradigm. We are in a period of transition. A new framework to give us direction which would carry conviction is not yet to hand, although the initial outline of a future paradigm has become discernible.

A paradigm shift is on the one hand a real break with the previous frame of reference, but a new paradigm is only seen to be reliable if it can provide explanation and confirmation, within newly defined boundaries, of the relative perceptions of truth contained in the old paradigm. The basic insights of the former paradigm must be incorporated into the new paradigm. Thus there is no going back on the discarding of the Christendom model with its sacralized concepts of order. The justified criticism of universalism must not lead to a legitimation of rampant ecclesiastical exclusiveness or provincialism. Similarly, the insight that the gospel applies to all areas of human life must not be obscured. The perception of the problems raised by taking salvation history and historical change as central categories of interpretaion must not lead to a surrender of human responsibility before allegedly autonomous "laws of nature".

All these challenges indicate that we must take yet more seriously the radical historicity of Christian existence in church and society. The decisive criticism of the former paradigm is that Christocentric universalism is unhistorical and dogmatic in nature.

The uncertainty and inconsistency of the situation of transition is also to be seen in the tendency to counter the life-threatening totalitarian claims of the economic, military-political, and scientific-technological system with the absolute claim of the lordship of the God of life. While this radical critical distinction between the powers of death and the God of life in concrete situations must continue to be made, it does not remove us from the realm of ambiguity. It is indeed questionable whether the liberating message of the gospel can still be expressed today in terms of "lordship" or "rule" or "dominion".

We are thus sent back into concrete history with all its contradictions and power struggles (which are not always manifestations of the "principalities and powers"), into the reality of human life as part of God's creation, into the facts of suffering and death as irremovable boundaries to human action in history. We are being pointed away from the concept of the cosmic Christ back to the historical Jesus and his deeds, in which, as parables, new life and the reality of the kingdom of God shine forth. And we are being pointed to the work of the Holy Spirit, who as the gift of the last days, shows up our world in its finitude, creates fellowship between the abidingly different, and precisely thus enables us to experience new life, life in its fullness.

# 4. The "Oikoumene": the One Household of Life

## 1. Further stimuli towards a new paradigm

Our analysis of the limits of the old paradigm when confronted with present challenges has in each case led to an attempt to formulate what we require and expect from a new paradigm. We shall now take up these tentative points to see if they can be connected and developed. Against this background three main emphases emerge as the starting point for our reflections:

— a Trinitarian understanding of the divine reality and of the relationship between God, the world and humankind;
— "life", understood as a web of reciprocal relationships, as a central point of reference (instead of history); and
— an understanding of the one church in each place and in all places as a fellowship in the sense of a community of those who are different from one another.

Each of these three areas lends itself to an approach taking relationships as its starting point, rather than structures or processes with specific goals.

Although, as far as I know, there have been up to now no other instances of an attempt to examine and interpret the present state of ecumenism by means of paradigm analysis, concern for a new common frame of reference has not been absent from ecumenical debate in recent years. Since these discussions have at least served indirectly as stimuli to the analysis I make here, they should be expressly mentioned at this point.

The *first* stimulus has come from the work of the Programme Guidelines Committee at the WCC Vancouver assembly in 1983. The committee formulated five guidelines for the work of the Council in the years to come and in this regard laid particular weight on "Growing Towards Vital and Coherent Theology". The report expressed this concern as follows:

> A vital theology will incorporate the rich diversity of theological approaches emerging out of the varied experiences of churches throughout the world. A coherent theological approach will incorporate tradition and methods of reflection which represent the concrete needs and call of each and all members of the ecumenical movement towards unity of life and faith. [1]

This recommendation had a particular background. The committee's task was, among other things, to examine the report of the central committee on the period between the Nairobi and Vancouver assemblies. It took as its basis the three programme guidelines formulated by the Nairobi assembly. With regard to the second of these guidelines on "The Incarnation of Our Faith" the committee came to the conclusion that:

> While attention to the interdependence of faith and life is evident throughout the report, it is also obvious that the appropriate tension between the two has not always been present, nor agreement reached on the nature of each element. [2]

The report continues:

> The theological diversity among the units and sub-units of the Council is perceived by some as a sign of vitality, by others as a sign of too little integration and too much division... The unconnectedness of unity of faith and unity of Christian life is also sharpened by the tension between growing confessionalism and conciliar unity. These strains in the interconnectedness envisioned in the guidelines hinder the embodiment of Christ's message of liberation and the dialogue with people of living faiths and ideologies. [3]

The concrete recommendation of the committee was the formation of a theological advisory group, which "would consider the place, diversity and interaction of theological work in all dimensions of the WCC through critical and constructive evaluation". [4]

The WCC central committee after the assembly did not for various reasons follow this specific recommendation to set up a theological advisory group. Instead, but completely in the spirit of the recommendation, a process of dialogue, taking various forms, was set in motion among the WCC staff with the assistance of some experienced colleagues from the churches.

From among the documentation on this internal debate on a "vital and coherent theology", I single out for particular mention here the report presented in February 1986 by José Míguez Bonino, of Argentina, after two and a half months of observant and reflective participation in the work in Geneva. His words carry particular weight because in Vancouver he was moderator of the Programme Guidelines Committee.

He attempts first of all to establish more clearly what is meant by "vital" and "coherent" theology. What is "coherence"?

> It is interesting to note that it is on this idea that the discussion has hinged. Vitality and diversity are taken for granted (perhaps too much for granted sometimes)... Coherence is related to things that are connected, internally related, having points of articulation. Only things that are different but related can co-inhere. But we need to move further.
>
> Coherence in the sense we are using it here should not be understood as the logical coherence of a systematic treatise or the mechanical coherence of a smoothly running machine. The coherence for which we may hope and work in the WCC — as a goal — is that of a living, growing organism...
>
> But within this organic understanding of coherence, vitality is necessary... But living organisms die when they become incoherent....[5]

The report then examines one by one the issues of a coherent theological framework, methodologies, and those responsible for theological work within the WCC, particularly in the Geneva office. Only the first cluster of issues is of interest here, although the similarity to the observations on the uncertainty in the ecumenical movement listed in chapter one is not accidental. With regard to the theological framework, Míguez Bonino expresses doubts whether the traditional Christological basis of the WCC is still adequate as a framework within which these diverse elements can find coherent inter-relation. He identifies three insufficiencies in particular:

— the lack of a clear Trinitarian perspective, which would enable us to overcome the tendency to Christomonism, give a coherent understanding of the dynamism of history and the relative autonomy of the "created world";
— concentration on a "Christology from the top", which does not give the humanity of Jesus Christ its full force; and
— the absence of an ecclesiology which would make it possible to reach an adequate understanding of the "ecclesial" significance of the WCC.[6]

The *second* stimulus has come out of the symposium on "Cultures in Dialogue" held in the autumn of 1984 to mark the end of Philip Potter's period of service as WCC general secretary. I have already referred several times to the report of the discussions at that symposium. As the sub-title of the report puts it, it was "a dialogue in the transit lounge of the ecumenical movement". In his introduction, Werner Simpfendörfer writes:

> The transit situation of the ecumenical movement was felt strongly by all
> who were present at Cartigny... None of the classical ecumenical issues were
> discussed in isolation, like unity, mission, service, education, which have
> become the official mandates of the WCC. They were all present, but in a sort
> of disguise, hidden in the new challenges that the WCC has faced for some
> years and which have led it on new and yet unexplored paths. The Cartigny
> agenda was *an agenda in transit*, because these three issues were no longer
> problems to be solved (as many of us had thought in former years!) but
> questions to be raised, to be asked in a critical and self-critical way: Is the "one
> earth" an "illusion" or a "promise"? Are we willing and able to pay "the price
> of cultural transformation" which a new community of men and women
> requires? Are "action and icon" reconcilable in a "sacramental ethics"? For me
> the basic significance of Cartigny is that it left the safe ground of ecumenical
> definitions, affirmations and conclusions and dared to enter the "transit
> lounge" of the ecumenical movement, to expose itself to the risks of dead-end
> roads, to unfinished business, in one word to the crisis of the ecumenical
> movement.[7]

The themes of the symposium dealt with three basic areas of ecumenical conflict: the conflict between North and South; the conflict between women and men; and the conflict between Eastern and Western Christianity. The last two, particularly, which are not explicitly dealt with here, complete the picture of internal inconsistency in the ecumenical situation. The aim of the symposium was, however, not to find "solutions", but to engage in the discipline of "cultures in dialogue" — a dialogue which is not simply a method, a means to an end beyond itself, but is the expression of an attitude of life, which forms relationships while respecting differences, in a situation of religious and cultural pluralism.

With the key phrase "cultures in dialogue" the symposium had taken up a basic element in the ecumenical thinking and action of Philip Potter. He had constantly described the future oikoumeme in the language of Hebrews and Revelation (Heb. 2:5; 13:14ff.; Rev. 21 and 22) as an open city, in which this universal dialogue of cultures can take place, as the earth which becomes one household *(oikos)*, in which all are open to one another, and can share a common life in all its inter-related diversity. He had frequently referred to Martin Buber's understanding of dialogue: "For him real life is meeting."[8] And he saw a welcome confirmation of this understanding of dialogue in the ecumenical "Guidelines on Dialogue with People of Living Faiths and Ideologies" where they declare:

> Dialogue, therefore, is a fundamental part of Christian service within community. In dialogue Christians actively respond to the command to "love God and your neighbour as yourself"... It is a joyful affirmation of life against chaos, and a participation with all who are allies of life in seeking the provisional goals of a better human community. [9]

Finally, the *third* stimulus has come out of my work with Philip Potter himself over many years. During his whole period of office as WCC general secretary he ceaselessly endeavoured to reflect on the clearly perceived crisis in the ecumenical movement and to formulate new perspectives for the future. The underlying concept to all these efforts was "fellowship" or "community" or "communion", beginning with his short speech after his election as general secretary in 1972, where he reflected on the cost of ecumenical fellowship, continuing through his reports to the central committee, and reaching a climax in his two major reports to the Nairobi and Vancouver assemblies. On many occasions he began from Paul's image of the body (1 Cor. 12) or the need to bear one another's burdens (Gal. 6:2ff.), and from this he developed the outline of a fellowship of openness, trust and suffering (1977); of co-inherence *(perichoresis)* in and with the Godhead and in and with one another (1979); a community of communication, faith, sharing, struggle for true human community, life and joy (1980); and, finally, a fellowship of healing and salvation (1981). [10]

Behind these contributions to the self-understanding of the WCC and the ecumenical movement, each of them related to particular contexts and situations, there was, of course, an overall vision, held with strong conviction, which Philip Potter spelt out connectedly in his report to the Vancouver assembly. [11] It has, I believe, lost none of its relevance, although it was hardly discussed at Vancouver. In it Potter examines one of the "images of life" from the pre-assembly Bible studies and develops his vision of the fellowship of the churches in the ecumenical movement in relation to 1 Peter 2:4ff. in an exposition of the image of "the house of living stones". He considers the whole range of meanings of the root "oikos" (house/household), such as ecology, economy, ecumenism; he examines the rich biblical testimony to the "house of Israel", the "house of God", the newly built house, of which Jesus Christ is the cornerstone, and, finally, the Christian community as a living house, still being built, as a sign of God's plan of salvation (oikonomia) to unite all peoples in justice and peace in one human family.

> It is this image and understanding of the living house which has motivated the ecumenical movement... The ecumenical movement is, therefore, the means by which the churches which form the house, the *oikos* of God, are seeking so to live and witness before all peoples that the whole *oikoumene* may become the *oikos* of God through the crucified and risen Christ in the power of the life-giving Spirit. [12]

He then incorporates into this framework the profile of the ecumenical fellowship of churches. The house, made up of the churches scattered throughout the world, is a fellowship of confessing, learning, participation, sharing, healing, reconciliation, unity and expectancy. Almost all the key words from his reports to the central committee over the previous ten years here reappear and are woven together into one related whole. Here the outline of a new paradigm is becoming discernible, which I shall now develop further together with the pointers and stimuli already mentioned.

## 2. The "oikoumene": the habitable earth

A new ecumenical paradigm would have to release a vision of the oikoumene which takes seriously the inconsistencies, conflicts and threats of the interdependent world situation and the historical diversity of the social forms taken by the church. For a start, it would be helpful to take up again our discussion on the meaning of the concept of "ecumenism". [13]

In 1951 the WCC central committee made an attempt at clarification:

> We would especially draw attention to the recent confusion in the use of the word "ecumenical". It is important to insist that this word, which comes from the Greek word for the whole inhabited earth, is properly used to describe everything that relates to the whole task of the whole church to bring the gospel to the whole world. It therefore covers equally the missionary movement and the movement towards unity, and must not be used to describe the latter in contradistinction to the former. [14]

Those involved in ecumenical debate since then have not always remained aware of this distinction. Thus in normal usage today we find two understandings of ecumenism existing side by side or even in opposition to each other. On the one hand, ecumenism is taken to refer exclusively to interchurch, interconfessional relationships, to efforts to achieve the "una sancta". This understanding is to be found above all in the Roman Catholic domain, and has been reinforced by the definition given of the "ecumenical movement" in the Decree on Ecumenism of the Second Vatican Council. [15] On the other hand, the emphasis is placed on the worldwide, universal meaning of ecumenism, its international or intercultural dimension. In these two contrasting understandings of ecumenism, the one referring to "the whole church" and the other referring to "the whole world", we see reflected the tangled history of the meaning of the word, and also the different experiences of the Christian churches. The Roman Catholic Church is itself a world church, universal in its orientation. From that perspective ecumenism is viewed as describing its relations with other Christian churches and communities. Most other churches in the ecumenical movement are constituted as local or territorial churches. For them the ecumenical movement is linked with the rediscovery of Christian universalism, the worldwide unity of the people of God and their mission to the whole world.

The distinction came to a head once again in the late 1960s in the confrontation between "church ecumenism" and "secular ecumenism". This led Philip Potter to take up afresh the question of our understanding of ecumenism in his first report as general secretary to the WCC central committee in 1973:

> Even more important is a *clearer understanding of "ecumenical"* as referring not only to the coming and being together of churches, but more biblically to "the whole inhabited earth" of men and women struggling to become what they were intended to be in the purpose of God. As the Psalmist affirms, in a liturgical setting: "The earth is the Lord's and all that is in it, the world *(oikoumene)* and they who dwell therein" (24:1). The ecumenical movement is thus seen to be wherever Christians and others are one way or another seeking to work for the unity of mankind. The churches participate in this movement in the full knowledge that the *oikoumene* is the Lord's and that he calls us to discern what he is doing among his creatures and in his creation on the basis and in the perspective of what he has done in Christ who is the centre of the ecumenical movement. Thus the search for the unity of the church is inextricably bound up with the struggle for the unity of mankind. [16]

That quotation provides yet another clear summary of Christocentric universalism as the ecumenical paradigm. It stands in clear continuity with the earlier definition of 1951. But it is not only this understanding of ecumenism that has since then experienced a crisis. If the perception which is being expressed in the sharp antithesis between a transnational oikoumene of domination and a Christian oikoumene of solidarity is even only approximately correct, then it must lead us to make critical distinctions in the traditional Christian understanding of ecumenism, in both its church-oriented and world-oriented forms.

The "oikoumene" then is not a description of a given state of affairs. It is not a matter of structures, but of dynamic, real relationships. When we say "oikoumene", we are not referring to a global abstraction, such as "one world", the "whole human race", or "one united world church". What we are speaking of are the actual and at the same time endangered connections and relationships between churches, between cultures, between people and human societies in their infinite variety, and between the world of humankind and creation as a whole. These connections are not self-evident, nor are they empirically verifiable, nor are they the result of subsequent rational or political linkages. All human beings in their living, knowing and acting are from the very beginning related to their world, to other people, to their living environment, to those things which are necessary to life. Being-in-relationship is as much a part of our nature as being-in-oneself. This is true of all living organisms, but it is especially true of human groups and social constructs, including the churches. Autonomy and interchange, selfhood and relationships condition each other. Human knowledge is accompanied by the quest for connections. But it does not create these connections, but rather perceives ever more comprehensively the original interconnectedness, which was there even before we are aware of it.

These basic considerations are also applicable to our understanding of the oikoumene. Out of the critical experience of radical change in the last two decades, which has affected both the relations of the churches with one another and the relations between societies, cultures and races, there has emerged a new awareness of the inhabited earth as an inter-related whole. When the one world is experienced as a closed system of domination and dependency, this awareness can be oppressive and paralyzing in its effects. This experience is not new. In the New Testament, particularly in the Book of Revelation, there is a critical perception of the imperial oikoumene of the Pax Romana as a threatening reality.[17] It has again become relevant today to recall this early Christian insight into the enigmatic ambiguity of the oikoumene in light of the power structure of the "transnational oikoumene", which is militarily secured, politically administered, economically organized and scientifically planned, which obeys a logic of power aiming at total control, and which increasingly stifles life and threatens to make the earth uninhabitable. By contrast the biblically based perception of the oikoumene proves to be a liberating impulse: it is founded on the totality of relationships, instead of structures; it is an expression of living interaction, instead of death-dealing autonomous laws. It lives in the certainty that the earth is habitable, because God has established his covenant for the whole of creation, and it is guided by the hope that God himself will dwell with humankind, with God's people. This closing vision of the Book of Revelation, which sees the future oikoumene coming down as a city from heaven, reveals the innermost core of the biblical understanding of oikoumene in the sense of the totality of relationships in community as it is revealed in the light of the End, from the perspective of the kingdom of God.

This qualitative understanding of the oikoumene as the one *habitable* earth amplifies and deepens the spatial, geographical perception of the *inhabited* earth. In the vision of Revelation there is at the same time an echo of the memory that the old oikoumene came into being as an extension of the ordered commonwealth of the ancient Greek polis to the entire territory of the Greco-Roman Empire. A pointer to the further development of this perspective of the oikoumene can be provided by the following words of Ernst Lange:

> The biblical promise has always been an "ecumenical" promise. The Christian conscience has to learn to adjust itself to the larger household to which it was from the very beginning "called out" and towards which it was from the very beginning directed, namely to the household of the whole inhabited earth. It has to be trained in a new sensibility, a new awareness of the world and time, or, rather in its own most original and basic sensibility. [18]

As far as I know Lange here introduces for the first time the key word "household" as a translation of "oikoumene". In the order of relationships within this household, what is decisive is "habitability", the sustainability, or capacity for survival, of the inhabited earth.

The oikoumene as a household, as an "oikos" — this metaphor is proving to be more and more clearly the point around which our thinking about a new paradigm is crystallizing. In his report to the Vancouver assembly, Philip Potter examined the various aspects of the biblical use of the image of "oikos". Jürgen Moltmann has sketched out "an ecological doctrine of creation", which views creation as the space for living of all living things, a space created and protected by God. [19] This and other suggestions have contributed to the wording of the overall title for this chapter "The Oikoumene: The One Household of Life". The oikoumene, understood as the one household of life created and preserved by God, thus extends beyond the world of humankind, of the one human race, to creation as a whole. The metaphor of the "household" (oikos) supersedes the narrow vision that sees history as the central category of interpretation. It reminds us that human history is bound up with the history of all living things and that the human household is incapable of surviving without being related to the other households which are its natural environment. The great household of the oikoumene includes a countless variety of small and very small households, which are related to one another and dependent on one another. Moltmann speaks of "the ecological concept of space", indicating thereby the basic truth that all living creatures obtain and shape the environment appropriate to them. [20] Animals and plants have their living space, which is specific to their species. Human beings have to create for themselves their space, their abode and dwelling place. Human life becomes possible only within such a protected space.

The "oikos" as "space for living" draws a boundary around itself, but at the same time enables relationships to be formed.

> The space of the living person is always enclosed space... But the enclosure of the space moulded by human life does not merely protect, and does not only repulse. At the same time it means the possibility of communication with neighbouring beings and their environments. It evokes neighbourliness... Every frontier enclosing the living space of a living thing is an open frontier. If it is closed, the living thing dies. The ownership of any given space, and the community of the living in the universal cohesion of communication, are not mutually exclusive. On the contrary, they are the very conditions which make one another possible. [21]

The "ecological" structure of the household of the oikoumene constantly displays this duality between boundary and openness, independence and relationship, rest and movement, the familiar and the alien, continuity and discontinuity.

Recent Old Testament research has convincingly demonstrated that this ecological interpretation of the inter-related spaces for living accords with the biblical understanding of creation. [22] This is also true of Israel's space for living, the land given in trust by God. The covenant, the Torah, can be seen as the "house rules" for the "house of Israel", the aim of which is to enable all members of the household to live a properly human life. It is above all an ordinance to protect the weaker members of the people, whose right to life is under threat. Just as in creation God's creative work and God's rest are related — on the sabbath of the seven days of creation

God rests, and thereby confers on creation an independent life — so also in the household of Israel the sabbath rest becomes an ordinance to protect slaves, animals, plants and the cultivated land. Those beings who have no defence against human intervention in their "households" have their right to an independent life periodically confirmed and are thus able to regain their strength for living. The extension of the sabbath regulation to social relationships within the household of Israel (the sabbath year and the year of jubilee) is intended to maintain the viability of the household of the people as a whole, since it protects the life of its weakest members. The sabbath thus becomes an eschatological symbol of the restored order of the household of the whole creation, which permits all creatures to live and dwell in peace (shalom).

As Israel's covenant partner God is the guarantor of the life ordinances of the household of Israel and of the whole creation. [23] God dwells in the "house of Israel" (Ex. 25:8). A rich varied complex of traditions grew up in Israel around the "dwelling of God", God's abiding presence. But not only the sanctuary or later the temple are the "house of God": Israel as a whole can be addressed as "God's house" (Hos. 8:1; 9:8,15; Jer. 12:7; Zech. 9:8). Later tradition speaks of the presence of God among his people and in creation in the personified form of the "shekinah" (the "presence"), and the Christian community witnesses to the indwelling, the presence, of God by the Spirit (1 Cor. 3:16; Rom. 8:9,11). Through the indwelling of the Spirit the community itself becomes a house, a dwelling for God (Eph. 2:19ff.; 1 Pet. 2:4ff.; Heb. 3:1ff.). The viability of the household, the ordering of relationships between its members, rests on God's indwelling. When God abandons the house, or is driven out of it, or is displaced by other gods, the house of freedom changes into a house of bondage. It is not only the oikoumene of "solidarity of living things" that has the structure of a household: so also does the oikoumene of domination. But in the latter, relationships between free and equal members of the household are changed into structures of subordination and dependency. That is why it is important that the liberating presence of God in the messianic proclamation of Jesus should not only be presented in the image of the "kingdom" or "rule" of God, but also in the form found in the parables of the father of a great household, the host at the feast. [24] Indeed, God, the master and owner of the house, takes on in Jesus Christ the form of a servant, a slave in the household, so as to be close to those who have been excluded from the "house of Israel". The central significance of God's name as "father" in the language of Jesus has often been emphasized: the image of the house or household is in keeping with talk of God as father, whereas the kingdom, rule, dominion belong to the language of kingship.[25] The metaphor of the "household of God" could thus help us to overcome the easily misunderstood ambiguity of talk of the "kingdom of God" or of the "lordship of Christ", all the more so as the traditional language describing our response to God's invitation to fellowship in God's kingdom/household uses above all the words "service" and "obedience".

The "household" metaphor also opens up a further understanding of the new status of the children of God: from being slaves and dependents in the house of bondage they become free persons and sons and daughters, i.e. members of God's household in their own right. Finally, the common meal is also associated with the "household" metaphor. The gathering of the scattered members of the household to share in a common meal in Jesus" parables can exactly epitomize God's dwelling with humankind (Matt. 22:1ff. and parallels; Luke 13:29; cf. Isa. 25:6ff.). In fact, Jesus' own meals with those on the periphery of Israel become a messianic anticipation of the promised fellowship in God's house.

The newly discovered quality of the fellowship of the household in Jesus' preaching and practice find expression in the summaries of Acts: the disciples remain together, they have all things in common, they break bread "from house to house" and joyfully share their meals (Acts 2:42ff.; 4:32ff.). The house or household structure of the early Christian community as God's extended family is also reflected in the use of the word "oikonomia" (administration of the household, welfare) to describe the principal form of service in the community, and when Ephesians (1:10; 3:9) speaks of God's plan of salvation as "oikonomia", that should ensure that we do not quickly forget the concrete care of the divine father for the whole household.[26]

These pointers will, I hope, suffice to make clear the various applications of the metaphor of the household and its significance for a fresh understanding of the oikoumene as the "household of life" created and preserved by God. In this metaphor, the ecological, social, political and ecclesiological dimensions of the oikoumene are linked in the closest way possible. Certainly the metaphor originates from the milieu of extended families in rural society and a social structure in which relatively independent "households" lived in ordered relationship with one another. But in the contemporary situation of increasing individualism and alienation on the one hand and the global interlocking of structures on the other, the metaphor can help to fill out the programmatic statement of the "oikoumene of solidarity" with concrete ideas and translate it into criteria for reaching judgments and taking action. In any case, the justified criticism of the patriarchal structure of the extended family in the ancient world and of its inclusion in the New Testament, e.g. in the "house tables", should not prevent us from discovering contemporary examples of "households" practising solidarity, such as the base communities. Finally, I wish to emphasize that the habitability, the viability of the household of the oikoumene depends on whether we can maintain the duality of our own space for living and shared life, of independence and relationship. The separate existence of one's own household and its relation to the larger household will be clarified yet further as the paradigm develops.

## 3. The divine society of the Trinity

The universalism of the old paradigm was emphatically Christocentric. The traditional Christology of incarnation and exaltation included in the WCC basis enabled us to see the universal significance of the Christ event, in which the idea of the "lordship of Christ over the world and the church" played a decisive role. At various times in the course of this analysis critical questions have been raised about this position, pointing out the danger that confession of the living Lord can become a Christocentric principle as the basis for a universal theology of history (Hendrikus Berkhof), or even that Christocentrism could surreptitiously change into Christomonism (Stanley Samartha). Criticism of the Christocentric orientation of the old paradigm has given rise to three challenges, which, taken together, make it necessary to root the ecumenical paradigm more firmly in the Trinity:

— the *theocentric* orientation of the biblical tradition, especially in the proclamation of Jesus, must be reasserted;
— it is high time that we developed a *concrete Christology*, using recent exegetical and particularly social-historical research in the New Testament, i.e. a Christology which takes seriously the historical context and practice of Jesus of Nazareth; and
— the constitutive significance of the *Spirit* in the biblical witness to God's saving work in Jesus Christ must be theologically recognized.

Formal acknowledgment of belief in the Trinity has, of course, never been a problem in the ecumenical movement, particularly since the basis was expanded at the New Delhi assembly to include the Trinity. But the Trinitarian doxology does not yet necessarily progress beyond an understanding of the Trinity as a formal principle of salvation history, which remains none the less unchanged in its Christocentric orientation. Intensive encounter with Orthodox traditions of theology and piety has made us aware of the deep-rooted "obliviousness to the Spirit" (Walter Kasper) in Western Christianity, both in its Catholic and Protestant forms. In particular, the connection between Christology and pneumatology (the *filioque* controversy) and the relation of the Spirit to the church have become subjects of intense debate.[27] Meanwhile, the recent ecumenical encounter between Eastern and Western traditions has led to a fundamental renewal of Trinitarian thinking and in particular to a rediscovery of the ancient church doctrine of *perichoresis*, i.e. the fellowship of the three persons of the Trinity in reciprocal interpenetration, as a basic category for discourse about God, for clarifying the relation between God and creation, and for anthropology and ecclesiology.[28] We have already been pointed to the social being of God by our development of the metaphor of the "household of creation", of God's indwelling through the Spirit, who builds the community into a "house of God". This has led us to an initial critical questioning of the traditional language of the "lordship of God": house and kingdom, father and king, indwelling/relationship and rule/ authority are in tension with each other. What is the relation between God as social being and God as ruler? This issue must now be taken up once again and examined more closely.

In the language of the "lordship of Christ" the tradition of theocracy lives on, particularly in its Calvinist form. Arend van Leeuwen saw the overcoming of "ontocracy" by "theocracy" as the completion of the process of secularization. Since its origins in the proclamation of the prophets of the Old Testament, the theocratic tradition has been first and foremost a critical movement against all forms of sacralized authority. Its place has been, and still is, above all in situations of persecution and conflict, i.e. it represents the perspective "from below". Its liberating thrust, which has as its aim a radical revaluation of all forms of authority, loses its force, however, where the lordship of God is invoked to legitimate political or ecclesiastical hierarchies and claims to authority. This began when the critical monotheism of the biblical tradition was combined in the third century with the philosophical political monotheism of the Greco-Roman state ideology, and its ecclesiastical continuation is to be seen in the "papal revolution" (E. Rosenstock) of the eleventh century. The critical potential of the theocratic tradition is in fact indispensable, as is shown by the struggle of the Confessing Church and the dispute surrounding contemporary theologies of liberation. Where, however, theocentric criticism goes no further than capping all absolute claims to authority with God's universal authority, or even makes the lordship of Jesus Christ a principle out of which to construct a universal theology of history, it remains caught in the logic of domination and loses the liberating impetus of the biblical prophetic tradition. With the exception of the Hussite and Waldensian movements, which continue active to this day, and the emergence of the "radical Reformation", which lives on in the small peace churches, invocation of theocracy has proved incapable and inadequate to bring about the liberation of the church from its Constantinian captivity. This dilemma has also dogged the ecumenical movement to the present day.

Our criticism must therefore go deeper and even question the transfer of the political-social category of "authority" or "power" to the acts of God. All authority structures are constituted with one individual at the apex of the authority pyramid. Even the theocratic tradition — and not only the form of sacralized absolute authority it stands against — thinks monarchically and monotheistically. In its classical expression, the unitary concept of God has led to the idea of one universal church and also one universal empire: one God — one emperor — one church — one empire. This basically monistic structure of unity thinking is still operative today and has been reaffirmed in the Christocentrism of the old ecumenical paradigm. The latent religious and political monotheism, especially in Western theological and ecclesiastical tradition, has thus been correctly identified as the core of the problem, and this has become the starting point for a renewal of Trinitarian thinking. Although it is historically questionable to what extent the development of full Trinitarian theology, particularly in the fourth-century Cappodocian fathers, took place in debate with the political monotheism of the Christian Byzantine empire, the social doctrine of the Trinity developed by Basil the Great and his followers up to John of Damascus is in its approach an anti-authoritarian theology of the freedom of God and of humankind. [29]

The Greek fathers were led to a social doctrine of the Trinity which considers the relationships in the communion between Father, Son and Spirit, because they, in contrast to the Latin tradition, took as their starting point the concrete biblical witness and not the philosophical question of the relationship of the divine unity to the divine Trinity. Recent Trinitarian theological thought adopts this approach in that it examines the origins of Trinitarian thought in the history of Jesus Christ. Thus, interest in a concrete Christology and in the essential relationship between Christology and pneumatology is combined with a Trinitarian theological approach.

In order to carry forward this thought process, it is decisively important to appreciate the novelty of Jesus' proclamation of the kingdom of God in comparison with contemporary apocalyptic and messianic movements. The gospels clearly show the contrast to the message of John the Baptist:

> John proclaims the coming kingdom as God's wrathful judgment on the sin of men and women, and calls for repentance in the final hour, offering baptism as the last hope of salvation; Jesus proclaims the coming kingdom as the kingdom of God's coming grace and mercy. He presents it, not through an accusation of sinners, but through the forgiveness of sins... For Jesus, the gospel of the kingdom is a messianic message of joy, not an apocalyptic threat to the world (Matt. 11:1ff).[30]

The reason for this obvious difference is that "Jesus knows and proclaims the Lord of the coming kingdom as his Father".[31] Thus the message of the kingdom of God is given a completely new quality:

> Jesus did not proclaim the kingdom of God *the Lord*, but the kingdom of God *his Father*. It is not that lordship is the mark of God's fatherhood, but the very reverse: God's fatherhood towards Jesus the Son is the mark of the lordship and kingdom which Jesus preaches. That gives the kingdom he proclaimed a new quality. The *basileia* only exists in the context of God's fatherhood. In this kingdom God is not the Lord; he is the merciful Father. In this kingdom there are no servants; there are only God's free children. In this kingdom what is required is not obedience and submission; it is love and free participation.[32]

In his unique relationship to God as his Father Jesus acknowledges himself to be the Son. He reveals God as the Father who seeks the lost and in his great mercy turns to those who are excluded from God's "house" (cf. esp. Luke 15). But this revelation of God the Father does not remain simply a new doctrine: in Jesus it becomes a new praxis. He acts in the name of the Father and himself enters into solidarity with the poor and despised of his people (Matt. 11:25ff.). In his action the eschatological symbol of the sabbath rest takes on concrete form (Luke 4:16ff.). Jesus' way inevitably leads him into confrontation with the centre of religious and political power, the Jerusalem temple. It becomes a struggle for the liberation and restoration of the "house of his Father" (Mark 11:1-13:2, and parallels). He dies on the cross "because not only was he breaking the sabbath but, by calling God his own Father, he was claiming equality with God" (John 5:18).

The discourses in the gospel of John express succinctly the communion of the Father and the Son. "The Father and I are one" (John 10:30).

"Anyone who has seen me has seen the Father" (John 14:9). Or, in the language of Jesus' high-priestly prayer, "You, Father, are in me, and I in you" (John 17:21). But Jesus does not cling to his exclusive relationship with God as his Father. The prayer which he teaches his disciples includes them in the relationship with God as Father, making them God's children. Among themselves they become a new family, no longer knowing any earthly fathers, but only God as the Father (Mark 3:31ff.; 10:28ff.; Matt. 23:9ff.). The revaluation of all authority structures which this brings about is explicitly declared in Mark 10:42ff.: "You know that... the recognized rulers lord it over their subjects, and the great make their authority felt. It shall not be so with you; among you, whoever wants to be great must be your servant."

The community of his first disciples experiences the resurrection of Jesus from the dead as the breaking in of the messianic age, as the work of the life-creating Spirit. They testify to the Spirit as the gift of the risen and exalted Christ and in the Spirit they acknowledge him as God's Son, the Messiah, upon whom the Spirit of God has rested from the beginning. Thus the community's witness to Christ is indissolubly linked with witness to the work of the Spirit, who proceeds from the Father and is also the gift of the exalted Lord. By the Spirit he is created and begotten (Luke 1:35; Matt. 1:18ff.); in baptism he is declared Son of God by the Spirit and invested in his messianic office (Mark 1:10ff.); he acts in the power of the Spirit (Luke 4:16ff.; Matt. 12:28); he is raised by the power of the Spirit (Rom. 1:4; 8:11) and in his exaltation himself becomes a life-giving Spirit (1 Cor. 15:45).

> In the Spirit, Jesus is the reality of the new creation. In the Spirit, he is the new Adam, who is completely open to God and humankind... Because from the beginning he was totally of the Spirit, he is for that reason (Luke 1:35) the Son of God. The Spirit is in Jesus Christ, although here in a unique way, the one who mediates God to humankind and humankind to God. [33]

This Spirit makes men and women God's sons and daughters, brothers and sisters of Jesus Christ the Son, and enables us to cry, "Abba! Father!" (Rom. 8:14ff.; Gal. 4:6).

The predominance of the monarchical monotheistic tradition, which was reinforced in the West by the substance ontology of classical metaphysics, has made it extraordinarily difficult to express adequately the union of differences in God which is rooted in the witness of the New Testament and in Christian piety. There is no need here to go into the complex history of the development of the doctrine of the Trinity. I follow the approach of Jürgen Moltmann and Leonardo Boff, who see in the concept of *perichoresis* (mutual interpenetration of the persons), which can be traced back to John of Damascus (d.750), the starting point for developing a social doctrine of the Trinity, which incorporates the liberating thrust of Jesus' proclamation of the "rule" or "lordship" of God his Father, and which is open to humankind and to the creation as a whole by the action of the Spirit.

> New Testament belief in the Trinity forces us to accept differences for what they are and to put forward a vision of God and the universe as open realities engaged in a life-process. Unity does not here mean negation of differences or the reduction of them all to One, but expresses the communion and interpenetration of different strands. [34]

The divine reality can thus be expressed as a communion of different persons who receive their personhood in their relationship with one another. The distinction of the persons is essential for communion within the Godhead, just as relationships are essential for personhood. The mystery of this divine communion is indicated in 1 John in the words: "God is love; those who dwell in love are dwelling in God, and God in them" (4:16).

This social understanding of the three-in-oneness of God carries forward the social metaphor of the "household of God" and makes it possible to focus it more sharply. For

> ...it is not the monarchy of a ruler that corresponds to the Triune God; it is the community of men and women, without privileges and without subjugation..., a community in which people are defined through their relations with one another and in their significance for one another, not in opposition to one another, in terms of power and possession...
>
> The Christian doctrine of the Trinity provides the intellectual means whereby to harmonize personality and sociality in the community of men and women, without sacrificing the one to the other. [35]

It enables us to avoid subjecting the fellowship of Christians in the church and the fellowship of Christian churches to monistic unitary ways of thinking, but to think of it as a being-in-relationship of those who remain distinct and different. Here lies the significance of the new framework of thought for the question of the "unity" of the church.

### 4. Eucharistic fellowship

Two points have thus far emerged around which our thoughts can crystallize for a possible future ecumenical paradigm: they are the "oikos" structure of the oikoumene and a social understanding of the Trinity. In both cases the core is the living tension between personhood and social being, between independence and relatedness, between having boundaries and being open, between identity and communication. The "household" as an open space for living and the communion of the Trinity as the reciprocal relatedness of those who remain distinct and different are symbols, holding two opposite poles together in tension. I shall now attempt to expand these lines of thought into the realm of ecclesiology. A useful clue in this direction is the phrase "eucharistic vision" which the Vancouver assembly in 1983 offered as a pointer to the ecumenical way towards the realization of the unity of the church.[36] It takes up the aim in the WCC constitution, which is "to call the churches to the goal of visible unity in one faith and in one eucharistic fellowship", but expands the perspective beyond the traditional questions of the unity of the church to "its full richness of diversity".[37]

Critical reflection on the role of "unity thinking" in the light of the doctrine of the Trinity reinforces our reservations concerning the use of the concept of "unity" to define the goal of the ecumenical movement. In fact, as has been shown, since New Delhi the concept of "fellowship" (or communion — koinonia, communio) has come to the fore with increasing force in ecumenical debate to give some content to what is intended by the abstract term "unity". Fellowship has become the key ecclesiological concept for work in the Commission on Faith and Order, as also in the documents of the Second Vatican Council. In that way the form of the church as "communion" or "fellowship" is explicitly anchored in its participation in the living, open communion of the triune God.[38]

In his speech to the Vancouver assembly, Philip Potter explicitly linked the form of the church as a fellowship with the metaphor of "house" or "household". This link could be further developed by pointing out that in the symbol of the "house" the stronger emphasis is on the institutional aspect, on structures, on what endures, on distinctive differences, whereas "fellowship" brings to the fore the dynamic, relational aspect. In the image of the "house of living stones" or in the metaphor used here of the "household", both aspects are linked together.

The rediscovery of the eucharistic theology of the ancient church has prepared the way for independent justification for using the concept of "fellowship" in the context of ecclesiology. This has been taking place simultaneously in East and West and has resulted in the emergence with increasing force of a "eucharistic ecclesiology" in ecumenical debate, a position which, admittedly, is still in some tension with traditional approaches.[39] This is true, not only of the churches of the Reformation, with their insistence on the pre-eminence of "the Word and faith", but also of Orthodox and Roman Catholic scholastic theology. However, the outline of a new ecclesiological frame of reference is here emerging, as many of the bilateral conversations in recent years have shown.

I shall now trace the essential basic features of eucharistic ecclesiology, following John Zizioulas. The key text is 1 Corinthians 10:16-17:

> When we bless the cup of blessing, is it not a means of sharing in the blood of Christ? When we break the bread, is it not a means of sharing in the body of Christ? Because there is one loaf, we, though many, are one body; for it is one loaf of which we all partake.

The decisive assertion is that the "many" become one body because they all share in the cup of blessing and the broken bread. Whenever the congregation gathers, comes together in one place (1 Cor. 11:18-20) to celebrate worship, the church is truly present as the gathering together of the scattered children of God (John 11:52). In very early days the prayer of the Didache incorporated this central thought of the gathering together of the many:

> As this broken bread was scattered upon the mountains, and being gathered together became one, so may your church be gathered together from the ends of the earth into your kingdom....[40]

And with regard to baptism, Paul elucidates what is meant by "the many":

> There is no such thing as Jew and Greek, slave and freeman, male and female; for you are all one person in Christ Jesus (Gal. 3:28).

The "many" is not only a reference to number: it refers to the whole variety of natural and social differences which are represented in the gathered congregation. Conversely, this means that when a congregation excludes people on grounds of differences of race, class or sex, it is an injury to the wholeness, the "catholicity" of the church.

What brings about the gathering together of those who are so different, with the result that Paul can say that they have all become one person (NB: one *person*) in Christ Jesus? The basis is not their brotherly or sisterly love, nor their solidarity with one another, nor their common belief, their confession of faith. Because they share in the one eucharistic bread, the sacramental body of Jesus Christ (1 Cor. 11:24), they *are*

Christ's body, the church. Whenever the many gather together to break the one bread, the eucharist makes real what is inaugurated in baptism:

> For in the one Spirit we were all brought into one body by baptism, whether Jews or Greeks, slaves or free; we were all given that one Spirit to drink (1 Cor. 12:13).

It is the work of the one Spirit that they become the one body of the church through sharing in the one eucharistic body of Christ. And the same Spirit who brings those who differ from one another together in the one body, so "constituting" the church (Zizioulas), transforms the various talents and conditions of human life into gifts and abilities which serve to build up the body of the church. Paul borrows the well-known organic metaphor of the body and its members from contemporary popular philosophy, but as the body of Christ the church is not simply an organism. Paul takes the organism as a simile ("Christ is like a single body...", 1 Cor. 12:12) to describe the quality of the congregation produced by the Spirit. It is not the members who constitute the body, but Christ and the Spirit. The congregation is the body of Christ by the power of the Spirit. The Spirit is not the "soul" of the body, which has been previously sacramentally constituted. Rather, the Spirit brings the church into being as a fellowship of those who are different from one another.

The pneumatic structure of communion in the body of Christ, in the church, is in direct accord with the pneumatic structure of the Christ event. In both, the Spirit is the power of a new creation, the gift of new life from God, the breaking in of the eschatological reality of the kingdom of God. Every celebration of the eucharist is thus an anticipation, a symbolic preview of the looked-for consummation in the kingdom of God. Every celebration of the eucharist takes place for the whole, as yet unredeemed, world. In every celebration the whole church is present in mutual intercession. In the bread and wine the creation itself is included in the symbolic eschatological transformation.

Participation in Jesus Christ in the eucharist means sharing his history. Jesus Christ assigns the church its place in history, i.e. among those with whom he had fellowship. The relation of the eucharist to Christ means that it can always only be celebrated in a particular place in the midst of all the differences which divide people from one another and make them dependent on one another. Eucharistic fellowship cannot be experienced in a corner, in a sheltered location away from the storms of life, but only in the midst of the contradictions and conflicts of actual human relationships, so as to reconcile them before the altar (Matt. 5:23ff.; 1 Cor.

11:20ff.). Indeed, it is only in the presence of Jesus Christ that the differences which divide are truly exposed.

Sharing in the one Spirit means sharing in the new creation in the eschatological power of new life. By the Spirit, differences are transformed into a reciprocal relationship of manifold gifts and ministries. But by the Spirit the "many" are brought together into a fellowship not only in each place: the same Spirit brings about the essential relationship of the congregation in each place with the congregations in all other places.[41] By the power of the Spirit, the body of Christ is a universal reality. This is shown by the fact that the New Testament only has one word for the local congregation and the universal church: "ecclesia". The link of the local with the universal is not a matter of structures. The local congregation is not simply a fragment of the universal church, nor is the whole church the sum-total of all the local churches. The whole church lives in the Spirit-produced relationship of the various local churches, which in themselves possess the complete fullness of life in Christ.

With this background, we can now resume consideration of the question of how we deal with diversity in the fellowship of the church and of what connection there is between our own household and the household of the whole of creation. In the life of every individual church or congregation, as in the life of the church as a whole, it is true that diversity, differences are a condition of fellowship. What we see is a constantly new gathering together of the many who are different into the one Spirit-produced community. We can indeed now go further: it is precisely the local concrete obligation arising out of sharing in the history of Jesus Christ, the task to proclaim the gospel of the kingdom of God as a concrete message of liberation and to enable it to take concrete form, which constantly produces fresh differences within and between congregations. These differences are not signs of a lack of unity, but signs of vitality in the body of Christ — provided that they do not erect exclusive boundaries between one another or infringe the essential inter-relatedness of the Spirit-produced community. The decisive criterion of ecclesial fellowship is the eucharist, which is celebrated in each place with and for the whole church. In the eucharist, our incorporation into Christ's universal body, which takes place in baptism by the power of the Spirit, is repeatedly made a present reality.

The church exists in this duality of the local fellowship and the universal church. The celebration of the eucharist links the local with the universal, and concrete, particular, contradictory history with the eschatological wholeness (shalom) of the new creation. To these two basic dimensions of the church, H. Dombois has assigned two further derivative forms of the church: the "intermediate" church, i.e. a structural linkage of various local churches in a particular culturally and historically delimited area; and "orders", i.e. committed communities of individual Christians.[42] This distinction has meanwhile been taken up and further developed in the direction of a description by type of four basic forms of the church. In addition to the local congregation, there is also the universal network, a federal or conciliar association of churches. As intermediate bodies there are regional churches and intentional groups.[43] While this analysis of various types of church is useful in critically questioning the monopoly claim of particular forms of the church, it does, however, shift the emphasis from the ecclesiological to the sociological plane. The primary issue here is, however, how to cope ecclesiologically with diversity and how to link the local with the universal.

According to Dombois, the task of "intermediate" churches is to mediate between the local and universal dimensions of the church, but they have no independent ecclesiological status, only a derivative status. They are a constant reminder that the universal church only lives in the concrete setting of a given culture and society and they point each local church to its essential inter-relation with those beyond the boundaries of its own "household". The "orders" — groups of committed followers, or base communities — are an embodiment in visible form of the gospel call to liberation from the cultural and social bondage of the church, which is a consequence of its excessive conformity. They advocate the commitment of discipleship, which comes into conflict with all historical conformity by the church to social structures and styles of authority. But they only have ecclesiological status to the extent that in their life and witness they remain in relation with the gathering of the many in one place, to show forth in the celebration of worship the one body of Christ, the one "household of God". Their role in the church is often precisely to point out the place where the church at present ought to be, at the points of tension in society, to draw attention to the failure of the church to be "localized", and to call upon it to "relocate" itself.

The administrative structures of the intermediate churches and the networks of committed Christians are, however, not independent "households of God" in themselves. A "household" is not constituted by a legally and politically safeguarded structural uniformity, nor by a common decision to commit oneself to a particular course of action, but by the coming together of those who remain distinct and different into a household community, in which there are no longer the pious and the worldly, the committed and the uncommitted, those who accept responsibilities and those who are simply members, but in which all have become "one person" in Jesus Christ through the indwelling of God's Spirit. It is precisely by attempting to change these differences originating in separation into building blocks of fellowship that the churches will serve the "unity of the church". Unity thus begins to become a reality at local level, and churches which are prepared to respond to this challenge of diversity in the power of the Spirit will have no problems with diversity in their relationships with one another in their various localities. The universal remains an eschatological reality, which only attains tangible form in being anticipated in eucharistic fellowship.

## 5. The ecumenical household

### 5.1. Aliens or members of the household

Together with the seventeenth chapter of John's Gospel, the Letter to the Ephesians is rightly reckoned to be the decisive New Testament foundation for all ecumenical talk of the "unity" of the church (cf. esp. Eph. 4:1-6). The vision of unity in Ephesians is linked from the beginning to the fundamental distinction between gentiles and Jews. The wall of division between "inside" and "outside" has been broken down by Jesus Christ by the sacrifice of his body (Eph. 2:14). The author, using language originating in early Christian baptismal discourses (dead-alive; formerly-now), states:

> Once you were far off, but now in union with Christ Jesus you have been brought near through the shedding of Christ's blood... Thus you are no longer aliens in a foreign land, but fellow-citizens with God's people, members of God's household. You are built on the foundation of the apostles and prophets, with Christ Jesus himself as the corner-stone (Eph. 2:13,19-20).

The congregation thus becomes a building, a "temple in the Lord", a dwelling for God in the Spirit (Eph. 2:21-22).

We find here again the multi-faceted metaphorical language of the house and the household (oikos). I shall develop it somewhat further in this last section, so as to make visible its significance for the practice of the ecumenical movement.

"Members of God's household" is the new honorific title of those who, together with the house of Israel, in baptism "have access to the Father in the one Spirit" (Eph. 2:18). They become a "household", a "dwelling" for

God in the Spirit. The phrase "membership of God's household" could thus be an aid to understanding what is meant by the Spirit-produced fellowship of those who are different, for what is being described here is not only "community" or "communion" or "fellowship" as we understand it today, but a new "commonwealth" (polis, *politeuma*), which includes all natural and social differences in human life, including the religious distinction between gentiles and Jews. The members of the household *(oikeioi)* are members of one household, one extended family, which includes the domestic slaves and servants. Alongside the household members there were the "resident aliens" *(paroikoi)*, or "sojourners", who were accorded explicit protection in the household of Israel (Exod. 22:21; Lev. 19:33ff.). Up to that moment gentile Christians had been aliens in God's household: now, however, through Jesus Christ they had become members with equal rights.

Every human house has its owner, its "lord of the house". Every household has its "house father", a "head of the household". But God's new extended family no longer knows any earthly fathers. The members of the household have been incorporated into one household, whose master made himself a slave, a servant in his own household in Jesus Christ. In this household, there is no master or father apart from God. Thus the patriarchal order of the house is abolished in a radical revaluation of relationships. Everyone exercising a function or "ministry" *(oikonomia)* in God's household does so as a steward. The householder *(oikonomos)* represents the lord of the house, and his task is caring *(oikonomia)* for the life of all members of the household. God has renounced the unlimited exercise of the divine right as lord of the house: he has made a covenant with God's house and committed himself to care for everyone in it. The covenant takes concrete form in the "house rules" (torah), which are designed to protect the right to life of all members of the household.

The metaphor of "membership of the household" to describe the relationship of the baptized to one another has advantage over the concepts of "partnership" or "brotherhood" or "sisterhood". Members of the household have equal rights and are yet different. They do not create the house themselves, but are incorporated into it, added to it. Even the weak, the dependent, the doubters and the uncommitted belong to God's household as full members. In the one house of the Father there are many "dwelling-places" (John 14:2), and not only *one* committed community. Membership of the household includes full participation for all members of the household. It refers to one concrete household, one locality, and thus forms part of the diverse relationships of the various households one to another, which is so essential to life. It does not remain an idea, an attitude or an opinion.

Just as the Letter to the Ephesians addresses those who were formerly "aliens" *(paroikoi)* as emphatically members of God's household and fellow-citizens in the commonwealth of the saints (cf. also Heb. 3:1-6; Gal. 6:10), so also does 1 Peter, from which the image of the "house of living stones" comes, speak naturally of Christians as now "aliens in a foreign land" (1 Pet. 2:11). Just as Abraham was an alien and lived in tents in the land which had been promised him (Heb. 11:9), because he was looking forward to the promised city to come (Heb. 11:10; 13:14), and just as Israel was constantly reminded that God chose the people "when they were still living as aliens in Egypt" (Acts 13:17) — so the congregation as a "household of God" knows itself to be "aliens in a foreign land", scattered in the "diaspora" (1 Pet. 1:1, 2:11; James 1:1). They were deeply conscious of this sense of the provisional nature of the historical existence of the community as life in a foreign land looking forward to the abode to come, as can be seen from the language used by the apostolic fathers and the following generations, who described the concrete church in a particular locality as a "paroikia" (our word "parish", cf. "parochial"), whereas the word "church" (ecclesia) was now used for the universal church. [44] While here — before the beginning of the Constantinian era — the awareness was still expressed that the universal remains an eschatological reality, which can be anticipated in history only in the power of the Spirit, the relationship was later reversed: the universal church with its centre in Rome became predominant, and the parish, from being the concrete location of God's indwelling in the Spirit, was transformed into the smallest unit, a particle of the universal church. And in the churches of the Reformation, their fixation on the parish, the "parochial captivity of the Christian conscience" (Lange) became a decisive obstacle to genuine ecumenical awareness. [45]

After the collapse of the "corpus Christianum", the ecumenical movement has begun to acknowledge afresh the provisional nature of the church in its diaspora existence. The transformation of the whole human race, of the creation as a whole into the "household of God" is the promise by which the church lives and the goal towards which its life is directed. Its task is not the Christianization of the oikoumene. Rather the church is to live as salt of the earth, as light of the world, and through its life be a visible witness to the new community in the household of God

(Matt. 5:13ff.). The church is to live for the world, is to change the world.

> Precisely because the church does not exist for itself, but completely and exclusively for the world, it is necessary that the church not become world, that it retain its own countenance.[46]

## 5.2. The "house rules" of God's household

The First Letter to the Corinthians in chapters 3ff. develops by means of concrete cases the "house rules" which apply in God's house. It addresses the community as God's building *(oikodome)*, whose foundation is Jesus Christ (1 Cor. 3:9-11), and as God's temple, where the Spirit of God dwells (1 Cor. 3:16). God's temple is, however, holy, and God's "house rules" apply within it. I shall now examine some of these basic rules by which the house is to be ordered, which are of particular importance for relationships between the churches in the ecumenical movement.

*Self-limitation and renunciation of violence:* The command to love and to refrain from violence even towards one's enemies is known from the Sermon on the Mount (Matt. 5:38ff. and 43ff.; Luke 6:27ff.). The early Christian communities understood this as a binding rule for life together in God's household. In this spirit, Paul in 1 Corinthians 3:18-4:13 gives his instructions to refrain from boasting and self-justification, and from passing judgment, actions which exclude those who live or think differently (cf. also Rom. 14 and 15). He declares particularly that "luxuriating in power and possessions" (C.F. von Weizsäcker) is the source of conflict (1 Cor 4:8) and confronts it with the pointed question: "What do you possess that was not given you?" (1 Cor. 4:7).

The church lives by the power of God's Spirit ever received afresh. The wholeness of the church remains an eschatological reality, which in history only takes concrete form in the multiplicity of actual "households" in each locality. Any form of the church remains provisional.

> [No church] is immersed in the secular to the point of no longer being capable of standing out from it; none has taken on the secular to the point of trans-substantiating it. But by their activities all tend to seek to abolish separation in order to hasten the hour of the kingdom: their mediation and their multiplicity keep them from succumbing to this temptation. For when they do succumb to it they use violence, and their actions, too conformed to the violence of history, make it evident that they are not identical with the kingdom. When they enter into ecumenical negotiation, their renunciation of violence ensures that they personally are identified with the kingdom. To

create a bond without exclusion suggests as a starting point a truth experienced as a limit but given as a hope. [47]

The relativizing of the truth claims of each church is the concrete form taken by the renunciation of violence in the ecumenical "household of God".

*Dialogue and striving for truth:* The household is a place for conversation, and the members of the household a community of communication. Dialogue between members of the household is not a method, a means to an end, but the most basic expression of their relationship. A household where the members no longer talk to one another is dead and decaying. Here I would recall what I said earlier on "cultures in dialogue". At Louvain in 1971 John Gatu quoted an African proverb: "To talk is to love"; and he added that the converse is also true: "To love is to talk". [48] Dialogue is thus the appropriate method to deal with conflicts between members of the household, a practical outwork-ing of non-violence. In 1 Corinthians 6 Paul instructs the congregation not to take their internal disputes before pagan courts. The chapters following deal with concrete disputes. John Zizioulas has reminded us of the earlier insight of Hans Lietzmann that these chapters of 1 Corinthians were appointed to be read at the eucharistic gathering of the congregation in the belief that the congregation gathered at the eucharist was the place where conflicts should be dealt with and resolved in dialogue. Zizioulas speaks of "primitive conciliarity" on the level of the local church. [49] Such dialogue between members of the household takes place

> in the belief that the Holy Spirit can use such meetings for his own purpose of reconciling, renewing and reforming the church by guiding it towards the fullness of truth and love. [50]

If dialogue is an expression of the basic relationship between members of the household, there are consequences for "ecumenical dialogue":

> The attempt of the churches to proceed via "dialogue" to "consensus" as a result of dialogue, so as then to be able to restore communion between the churches, is contrived and remote from life, in that communion does not come into being and is not experienced at all in that way. In these successive stages — first, dialogue; then, consensus; and then finally, communion — what is overlooked is that dialogue *is* living communion. Communion, fellowship, without dialogue is dead. Dialogue is not a means to an end: it is rather living communion itself. [51]

If dialogue between members of the household is thus recognized again as the living centre of the household of God, then the ministry takes on a new role as the stimulator and "moderator" of dialogue:

> The authority of this ministry is shown in careful listening and in enabling everyone to speak and hear in such a way that true dialogue can take place.[52]

*Sharing in solidarity:* Sharing what is necessary to life and standing by one another in solidarity are two of the basic requirements for living in any household or family. The relations between members of the household obey a different logic from that prevailing between social, economic and political structures: instead of the logic of power and the defence of property, the ruling logic here is the logic of solidarity and sharing. Many pre-industrial, agrarian cultures, particularly in Africa and Asia, still live following this rule. It has been rediscovered by the base communities of the poor in Latin America, and even the modern nuclear family can only survive as long as it obeys this fundamental logic of human life. When the congregation is therefore addressed as "the household of God", it is claimed to be a community of people who support and protect one another: it is by sharing that life increases. The presence of God's rule in the person of Jesus takes symbolic form in the feeding of the five thousand, as an act of sharing, in which all were satisfied (Matt. 14:13ff. and parallels; John 6:1ff.).

The Christian congregation has its origin in the primal act of sharing which comes from God. God's self-communication is recalled in every act of worship, especially in the celebration of the eucharist. Bearing one another's burdens (Gal. 6:2), sharing joys and sorrows (2 Cor. 1:1-2:4), and sharing want and abundance (2 Cor. 8:13ff.) are basic features of the life of the household both within and between congregations. The description of the first Christian congregation in Acts 2:42ff. and 4:32ff. may be an idealization of historical reality, but until the fourth and fifth centuries the obligation to share within the household of God was understood to be a binding rule. And the statement in Acts 4:34 that "there was never a needy person among them" is explicitly corroborated by later contemporaries.[53]

Sharing in solidarity in the church has been traditionally expressed by the concept of "stewardship" (cf. Luke 12:41ff.). After centuries of self-sufficient isolation, the ecumenical movement has made the churches aware once again of the obligation to share and to be in solidarity with one another.

It here becomes painfully evident how little the churches live as members of the one "household of God", in which goods and gifts are given for the benefit of all (1 Cor. 12:1ff.). In discussion on ecumenical diakonia, it has taken a long time to move forward from the classical idea of "aid" for those in need to a deeper understanding of ecumenical sharing.[54] For

> ...the ultimate aim of sharing is not to avert need, nor to achieve a fairer distribution of resources, but to build up Christian community, locally and throughout the world, as a sign of hope for humankind.[55]

A decisive obstacle to genuine sharing is the logic of power, which affects the way that even church structures behave.

> The sharing of material and human resources is a costly ministry because it entails the sharing of power.[56]

That is the principal challenge facing ecumenical stewardship today.

*Ecumenical learning:* Every household has a tendency to close in on itself. Every human group is inherently prone to exclude others. The history and the present of the Christian churches provide ample proof that the congregation constituted as the "household of God" also constantly succumbs to this danger and denies its fundamental relatedness and openness. Even after at least sixty years of the ecumenical movement, the task still remains, as Ernst Lange puts it in the article from which I have already quoted, that "the Christian conscience has to learn to adjust itself to the larger household... of the whole inhabited earth". Prompted by Lange, the insight has emerged that the ecumenical movement can by and large be understood as an open, never complete, learning process. Ecumenical learning thus means entering into the life of this larger household, which is in itself an interconnected web of small and very small households which are dependent on one another. The popular view of local and global as opposites is a paralyzing abstraction. Ecumenical learning does not mean absorbing items of information about global problems! This misunderstanding and the sense of total responsibility for the world deriving from it have led to that defensive blocking of awareness which is frequently complained about in discussions on ecumenical learning. Ecumenical learning is not primarily a matter of information, but of experience, i.e. it begins with individual experience of the distinctive differences of another household and aims at establishing connections. Precisely the experience of conflicts and contradictions, the discovery that everyday life situations are not all at the same stage of development, can set off processes of ecumenical learning. The attendant uncertainty and threat to one's traditional identity can be transformed through the hope of Christian faith into productive enthusiasm for learning. The basic place for making these connections is worship, especially in the world-embracing intercessions of the congregation and the celebration of the eucharist. What every celebration of the eucharist recalls and anticipates is spelt out in the lifelong process of ecumenical learning. Learning also means experiencing the goodness, truth, righteousness and peace of God, as they have become visible in Jesus Christ, and, by entering into this global context of all life, to contribute to the world's becoming the one household of God.[57]

### 5.3. Ecumenical hospitality

The fellowship of the members of the household, the extended family, is most intensively experienced and visible in the common meal. As it still is today in many cultures, in the whole biblical tradition eating together is an expression of the desire for fellowship. Thus the eschatological Day of the Lord, which inaugurates direct communion between God and humankind, is also described symbolically as a meal (Isa. 25:6; Zeph. 1:7; Luke 13:29; 14:15; Rev. 3:20; 19:9). Jesus' messianic meals with the "tax-collecters and sinners" (Mark 2:15ff. and parallels) are a foretaste of the great feast in the kingdom of God (Matt. 22:1ff.; Luke 14:16ff.). The hospitality Jesus deliberately showed to those who were excluded from the temple and the religious community of his day (cf. also Luke 14:21 — the invitation to the poor, the crippled, the blind and the lame) underlines the open invitation to salvation extended precisely to those who were "lost" (Luke 15:2 and the following parables). Thus "eating together" *(synesthien)* becomes a central symbolic word for membership in God's household.[58] The decisive importance of "eating together" is emphasized by the well-known disputes concerning granting or withholding table fellowship (Gal. 2:6ff.; Acts 10 and 11, esp. 11:3). For Paul, in the issue of table fellowship between gentile and Jewish Christians the whole of the faith in the justifying grace of God in Jesus Christ is at stake (Gal. 2:16). But it is also part of the practice of the faith to avoid or break off table fellowship with those who manifestly offend against God's will and reject the invitation to mend their ways (1 Cor. 5:9ff.; cf. also Matt. 22:11ff.). This has again become an acute issue today with regard to racism as a blatant offence against the will of God.

The meal of the members of God's household is the eucharist. Its nature as a fellowship meal has actually been rediscovered in the ecumenical movement. Here reference should be made once again to 1 Corinthians. In 11:17ff. Paul takes the Corinthians to task because the affluent members of the congregation are failing in their duty to show hospitality to the poor and the dependent slaves. This applies not only to the actual meal *(agape)*, but also to the eucharistic meal itself (1 Cor. 11:20,29,34). They become guilty of offending against the body and blood of the Lord and eat and drink judgment on themselves (1 Cor. 11:27-29). Since the time of the ancient church, granting or withholding eucharistic fellowship has been the decisive symbol of communion in the church. Jesus' open hospitality to the "tax-collectors and sinners" has admittedly been progressively lost, and it has even been forgotten that the ground of fellowship can only be faith in Jesus Christ (Gal. 2:16). The granting of table fellowship came to depend on more and more exclusive criteria. The church gradually ceased to be an "open system", which is what it should be by its very nature.[59]

The question as to how eucharistic fellowship between the churches can be recovered is at the centre of ecumenical debate. Meanwhile, it is clear that fellowship in the celebration of the eucharist should not be made a means, an instrument, in order to bring about intercommunion between the churches. In fact, "intercommunion" is not a helpful term. The eucharistic meal is the visible and sufficient expression of communion in the body of Christ. But the author and guarantor of this communion is God alone, who in Jesus Christ invites all men and women into the fellowship of God's children. The fellowship of the members of God's household is based on their being incorporated into the body of Christ, God's building, by confessing Jesus Christ and being baptized in the power of the Spirit. There is thus no reason for refusing fellowship in the Lord's supper to those who have opened themselves to the working of God's Spirit by confession of faith and baptism.

If we proceed on the basis that all the baptized are members in the household founded on Jesus Christ and brought about by God's Spirit, then no justification is required for granting hospitality in worship and in the celebration of the eucharist: it is the refusal of such hospitality that requires justification.

> Those who celebrate worship and share its meaning can wish for nothing else than to recover communion in worship with the other Christian churches. It is not the restoring of fellowship in worship that requires justifying, but the continuing to withhold it, because withholding it of itself contradicts the intention of worship, whereas restoring it is in accord with that intention.[60]

The eucharistic service celebrated at the WCC assembly at Vancouver following the "Lima liturgy" under the presidency of the archbishop of Canterbury was an impressive sign of this growing ecumenical hospitality, which gratefully accepts the gift of communion in Jesus Christ so as to grow in it and share it with all who accept God's invitation to the Supper in God's house. A most vivid image of such hospitality is Andrey Rublev's icon of the Trinity. The hospitality shown by Abraham to the three men (Gen. 18:1-8) becomes a symbol of the dwelling of the triune God in God's house in the form of the eucharistic meal.

> The cup, which in the Orthodox tradition contains both the bread and the wine, is the central message of this icon for the life of the world. The lack of daily bread, for which Christ taught us to pray, brings hunger, starvation and death to a world that is now unjustly divided between the rich and the poor. Here is the meeting of ecumenics and economics. The eucharistic cup calls for a daily sharing of bread and of material and spiritual resources with the millions of hungry people in this world. Through them God, the Trinity, comes on pilgrimage to us at every moment. [61]

# 5. Two Areas
## of Paradigm Shift

Out of the initially tentative thoughts in the preceding chapter the outline of a new paradigm has emerged with surprising clarity. It has also become clear that this new framework for orientation has already been at work subliminally for some time. Many of the basic elements of the paradigm we have identified are already familiar as key words in recent ecumenical debate. It could thus be asked how "new" this new paradigm after all is! The analysis presented here would, of course, have achieved its aim if it had succeeded in proving that the transition to a new paradigm had already taken place. For that it would be necessary to examine the inter-relation of the individual elements and the resultant consequences for a changed self-understanding of the ecumenical movement.

A systematic development of the approach taken here would have now to attempt to demonstrate how the new framework for orientation could do justice to the challenges to ecumenical universalism I have outlined, while at the same time being able to incorporate the truth of the central convictions of the old paradigm. That exercise cannot be taken any further here. And also the more far-reaching expectation — namely, to show that the new paradigm can make a decisive contribution to overcoming the uncertainty in the ecumenical movement I described in chapter I — cannot at this stage be fulfilled.

I shall, however, attempt briefly to take two selected current issues in ecumenical debate as test samples. They are, first, the question of "the ecclesiological significance of the WCC", which has recently been raised again, and, secondly, the initial stages of the "conciliar process for justice, peace and the integrity of creation". Both these areas of discussion, which are closely connected, provide a clear instance of the dilemma confronting the ecumenical movement.

## 1. The ecclesiological significance of the WCC

In the years following the Vancouver assembly the issue of the ecclesiological significance of the WCC, particularly in its relations with the Roman Catholic Church, has again been raised. What is the self-understanding of the WCC as a fellowship of churches in comparison with the Roman Catholic Church, which is a world church with a centralized structure? Is it possible for the WCC in the long run to act at world level as a partner of the Roman Catholic Church, to promote cooperation in concrete programmatic areas, and also accept that it appears as the world fellowship of the "non-Roman" churches? Does it not have to press for the complete universalization of the ecumenical fellowship?

The Toronto statement of 1950 on the ecclesiological significance of the WCC was drawn up at a time when the present extent of common ground and cooperation with the Roman Catholic Church would have seemed inconceivable. But also within the WCC fellowship of churches great changes have taken place. All attempts hitherto, however, to adapt the declarations of the Toronto statement to changed circumstances have seemed doomed to failure. Thus things remained the same for a further twenty years as they were described by W.A. Visser 't Hooft in his concluding remarks at the end of his paper to the WCC central committee in 1963 on "The Meaning of Membership in the World Council":

> It is better to live with a reality which transcends definition than to live with a definition which claims more substance than exists in reality.[1]

The attempt to state the "common ground" in the fourth official report of the Joint Working Group between the Roman Catholic Church and the World Council of Churches also produced no tangible results. It contains, however, the following noteworthy sentences:

> Despite all divisions which have occurred in the course of the centuries, there is a real though imperfect communion which continues to exist between those who believe in Christ and are baptized in his name... The ecumenical movement is therefore the common rediscovery of that existing reality and equally the common effort to overcome the obstacles standing in the way of perfect ecclesial communion... The nature of the communion by which we are held together cannot yet be described together in concrete terms. The language we use is marked by the divisions of history. Each church has its own approach and its own ecclesiological terminology. But since the churches meet in Christ's name and share in his gift, their fellowship must have ecclesial reality.[2]

Finally the attempt by Philip Potter in his general secretary's report to the WCC Vancouver assembly to reopen the debate on the "nature and calling" of the churches and the WCC similarly found no response:

> Certainly, Peter's image of the house of living stones reminds us of the inescapable fact that it is only as the churches relate to each other as living stones that they will discover new realities about their essential calling to be the church, the house of the Triune God. And this common calling demands a fellowship of confessing, learning, participating, sharing, healing, reconciliation, unity and expectancy, to the glory of God, Father, Son and Holy Spirit. The task of the World Council of Churches, as well as of regional and local councils, is to promote this common calling.

Potter then urged the assembly afresh together

> [to] advance to a new covenant relationship between the member churches at all levels of their life and the World Council at all levels of its activities.[3]

One looks in vain, however, for a real response to this initiative in the deliberations and decisions of the assembly, apart perhaps from the proposal, which I shall examine in the next section, for a conciliar process with the aim of a "covenant" for justice, peace and the integrity of creation.

While resistance to any development of the Toronto statement in the direction of a stronger emphasis on the ecclesiological significance of the WCC has come particularly from the Orthodox churches, yet the "neutral" position of the Toronto statement was invoked in the provisional response to the desire of the Orthodox WCC member churches to include a reference to baptism in the basis of the Council or at least in the criteria for admission of new members.[4]

That could have been an important step towards a more binding ecclesiological foundation for the WCC. After considerable discussion the decision was, however, taken simply to refer the matter to the Commission on Faith and Order for further study in the context of the reception process of the convergence document on *Baptism, Eucharist and Ministry*.

It was thus all the more surprising when, of all people, a Roman Catholic theologian who had been ecumenically committed for many years, Thomas Stransky, at the end of an article on relations between the Roman Catholic Church and the WCC, raised the question of "A Basis Beyond *the Basis*".[5] His reflections, following on from the statements on "the common ground" quoted in the above extracts, culminated in a suggestion to produce, analogously to the 1982 *Ecumenical Affirmation on Mission and Evangelism*, a "common ground" affirmation on "The Ecumenical Movement, the Church and the Churches, and the World Council of Churches". He continued:

> The Toronto document is out of date. True, many of its affirmations about what the WCC is *not*, about what membership in the WCC does *not* imply, are still valid and need reaffirmation. But a 1950 statement cannot be expected to do justice to the collective experience of the churches in the ecumenical movement since 1950, whether they be member churches or not... The Toronto document does not reflect what we today are perceiving our common calling is for, and to what we are called... I plea for a basis beyond the Basis, limited to be sure, but at least not a neutral ecclesiological stance towards the ecclesial implications of the Basis and the reflections of our common ecumenical experience... [6]

But what could the contents of such an affirmation be? Are there categories to describe the actual ecclesiological significance of the WCC? The reflections on the catholicity and apostolicity of the church and on the unity of the church in eucharistic and conciliar fellowship have been attempts in this direction. But they have got bogged down in the growing tendency to hark back to an older institutional ecclesiology. Any attempt to take the positive features of church structures as criteria for ecclesiological self-understanding is bound to fail as a way of defining the ecclesial nature of the ecumenical movement and the WCC as its privileged instrument.

But perhaps the question itself is already a dead-end road in that it gives in to the temptation to regard even the WCC as above all an institution at world level in potential competition with existing church institutions. The Roman Catholic Church and the Orthodox churches in particular have always reacted with extraordinary sensitivity to any attempt to ascribe ecclesiological nature to the WCC itself. So the question should in fact perhaps better be rephrased: is the fellowship that has grown up between the churches in the ecumenical movement ecclesial in nature and how can it be described? In any case, it is becoming increasingly clear that the rediscovery of the form of the church as a fellowship brought about by God's Spirit presents a basic challenge to the institutional, i.e. sacramental-hierarchical or organizational self-understanding of the majority of the WCC member churches. Perhaps the ecclesiological significance of the WCC shows itself precisely in that it opens up to the churches dimensions of their being as church which they would not know in isolation from one another. All traditional ecclesiologies are marked by their history of separation and isolation. Thus traditional ecclesiological criteria are inadequate to describe the WCC, which is a structure without precedent in the history of the church.

In any case, these considerations confirm the insight that relations with other churches as members of the ecumenical household or in conciliar fellowship belong inalienably to the *esse* of the church. No church can be church in the full meaning of the word apart from the other churches. For the WCC, this means that its ecclesiological self-limitation, which relies only on its power to convince, on the truth and wisdom which inform its statements and initiatives and claims no institutional authority, is not a declaration of powerlessness, but rather the only appropriate expression for the fellowship of the church at world level. The ecclesiological significance of the WCC lies precisely in that it is an instrument of this fellowship in reliance on the working of the Holy Spirit and thus participates in its ecclesial nature. All ecclesiological statements about the WCC can then, strictly speaking, be only statements about the quality of this fellowship between the churches. Thus it has been and still is true that the WCC must work towards the day when the churches will be in a position to express their essential relatedness in its full sense as conciliar fellowship, thus making the WCC redundant in its present form.

The fellowship achieved between the churches is not simply the result of persistent ecumenical labour. It must be seen as the work of the Holy Spirit, who is bringing the churches together beyond all differences in doctrine and church order and has made them aware afresh that they belong to the worldwide body of Christ. That brings us back once again to baptism. Despite the divisions in the history of the church, nearly all churches have preserved the bond of baptism. They believe that baptism as the act of incorporation into the body of Christ by the power of the Holy Spirit creates an invisible bond of fellowship between them, which is antecedent to any profession of faith or action by the churches. The WCC basis in its present version is limited to confession of Jesus Christ. If it were expanded or supplemented in accordance with the Orthodox proposal by mention of the one baptism, then the basis would say everything needful to describe the ecclesial nature of this fellowship of the churches. Confession of Jesus Christ and baptism are the visible signs of the fellowship, which is antecedent to all our ecumenical efforts to make visible the unity of the church.

It is difficult to say whether such an expanded basis and a corresponding revision of the Toronto statement would succeed in dispelling the reservations of the Roman Catholic Church to WCC membership. But at least that would mean that an ecclesiological foundation had been formulated which would reject even more decisively than the Toronto statement the universalist temptations of the "super-church" idea, in that it would root the eschatological and pneumatological nature of the universal fellowship of the churches explicitly in baptism. That would free the WCC from the dilemma of wishing that the Roman Catholic Church were a member church while at the same time coming repeatedly into unavoidable conflict with the form of the global unity of the church which Rome stands for.

That would, of course, make the "conciliar process for justice, peace and the integrity of creation" initiated by the Vancouver assembly all the more important. For precisely in this regard the question of the ecclesiological significance of the WCC vis-a-vis the Roman Catholic Church has come up again. It has arisen because of the Vatican decision to decline the invitation to co-sponsor the conciliar process and the world convocation, and in particular the reason given for the decision, which explicitly refers to the diverse nature of the two bodies, viz. the Roman Catholic Church and the WCC. This refusal, while regrettable, could help us to reach a clearer definition of the intention of the conciliar process. This process perhaps provides precisely the opportunity for the churches to be able to experience and strengthen the ecclesial nature of the fellowship between them, while leaving behind them the temptations to ecumenical universalism.

## 2. The conciliar process for justice, peace and the integrity of creation

We shall first recall its historical background. The WCC Vancouver assembly decided that one of the priorities for the Council's future work should be "to engage member churches in a conciliar process of mutual commitment (covenant) to justice, peace and the integrity of all creation".[7] This decision produced an unexpectedly widespread response, and also caused the WCC considerable embarrassment, because the coded wording clearly contained the hope for a sort of conciliar act of confession, a solemn act of commitment by the Christian churches.[8] But was it possible for the WCC to initiate and promote such a process with such obviously ecclesiological implications? The embarrassment increased when the Düsseldorf Kirchentag in 1985 took up the call for an ecumenical peace council in which all churches, including the Roman Catholic Church in particular, would participate.

Meanwhile it has become clear that, at least for the time being, the outcome will not be an ecumenical peace council. In a way, the discussion following the Uppsala assembly in 1968, which also spoke of a "genuinely universal council", has been repeated. Instead, the phrase "conciliar process" has emerged, and the WCC held a world convocation in 1990 on the urgent problems of justice, peace and the integrity of creation. The Roman Catholic Church participated in the convocation, but declined the request to be co-sponsor.

Despite these disappointments, concrete hopes for an ecumenical council persist. They obviously reflect a deep desire for an achievable ecumenical vision, and, they have, at least in the setting of Europe, given new impetus to ecumenical work at all levels of the church. The "conciliar process" by contrast remains comparatively abstract and vague: it excites interest only to the extent that it will lead to an authoritative act establishing a consensus among the churches, including the Roman Catholic Church, and making an unambiguous confession by the Christian community including specific condemnations. The thought of a council has fanned the glowing embers of the old ecumenical universalism into flame again, either in the form of hope for a universal unification of the churches, or in the form of keen expectation for a word "which humankind cannot fail to hear". We may here detect echoes of a certain fascination with the universal image projected by the Roman Catholic Church, and certainly the great councils of the ancient church were the early visible form of a global unity of the church. But can we today take up this tradition of authoritative councils simply where it left off? Our critical analysis of Christian universalism and the reminder that global union is the eschatological work of the Spirit should counsel caution here.

It is thus not surprising that the initial attempt to link the conciliar process for justice, peace and the integrity of creation directly with steps towards the unity of the church in conciliar fellowship had very early to be given up: it led only to increased reservations on the part of the Roman Catholic Church and the Orthodox churches. What still remains of the original vision is not able to inspire much enthusiasm. The main characteristic of the conciliar process seems to be that an almost countless number of committees and working groups are making preparations for a never-ending series of forums, meetings and conferences! The established churches have taken over responsibility for the process, and those who saw the distinctive feature of the conciliar process to be widespread participation by the people of God at all levels of church life feel deceived or are fighting for the right to have their say in the process.

Again we are confronted with an almost insurmountable barrier. If we discard our fixation on authoritative pronouncements, then it becomes clear that the aim of the conciliar process cannot be the harmony of a *magnus consensus*, nor the deceptive compromise of the lowest common denominator, and certainly not an unambiguous act of prophetic witness, but only a hard slog in the fellowship of those who are baptized into Christ and believe in him to bring about concrete embodiments of the gospel. The bond and inspiration of Christians and churches in the conciliar process is not a unity of the like-minded, but the fellowship of those who mutually correct one another as they seek the place of the church in today's world. Conciliar gatherings are thus the decisive points of intersection where insights gained in striving for the truth crystallize. But all the weight and authority they command is owing to the preceding and succeeding conciliar process. This experience has been confirmed many times over in the history of WCC assemblies.

It thus follows that in initiating a conciliar process it is more important to ask the right questions than to produce agreed answers. The questions, the problem indicators, are an expression of the incomplete and controversial nature of our perception of reality, and they also teach us to listen afresh to the witness of the Bible. Only a church which has gone through this mutual questioning in the conciliar process will have something to say to humankind and the world.

It may be that this conciliar process, which is already under way, if it really allows space for striving for the truth of the gospel and for giving a concrete contemporary confession by the church, will move towards a representative world conciliar gathering. It may also be that some of the gatherings organized at various levels in preparation for the 1990 world convocation may prove to have a truly conciliar quality, i.e. their pronouncements will be heard as words through which the spirit of the gospel, God's Spirit, is speaking. However different from one another, however inconsistent with one another the churches may be in their witness to the gospel, the fellowship created by God's Spirit endures, as long as the churches can acknowledge the voice and Spirit of Jesus Christ in the stance, testimony and action of each of the others.

This mutual recognition in striving to move forward from opposing positions is the inner mystery of the conciliar process.

So as to make this recognition more certain, the churches have formulated "touchstones" or "waymarks" in their conciliar history. These are as it were aids to translation so that communication can take place in the midst of differences and contradictions. Each generation produces further formulations to these guiding markers. The first ones, the canon of holy scripture and the rule of faith, were established in an open process without conciliar actions. The same is more or less the case, in different circumstances, with the ecumenical denial of racism, which has led the church to make a "preferential option" for the victims of racism in the struggle to achieve elementary justice. The conciliar process needs to be directed towards formulating such "touchstones", such guiding markers in face of the challenges of justice, peace and the integrity of creation.

But such touchstones and criteria for the churches' witness and service are then not the product of superior conciliar authority and certainly not the result of conclusive deductions from general statements of faith. They are rather the result of insights gained in striving for the truth. They remain provisional, revisable, and depend on being received in the fellowship of believers in Christ and on their truth being constantly tested.

What distinguishes the present process from earlier phases of committed ecumenical dialogue is not the (deceptive) hope for a universal council which will finally settle all contentious issues, but on the one hand a changed perception of reality, which requires us to ask new, wider-ranging questions, and on the other hand the insight that many of the already formulated norms are inter-related and are crying out to be expressed in a comprehensive articulated way, and linked afresh with the underlying biblical witness. That does not mean that a pronouncement will be made after a long process of conciliar deliberation. But it does amount to a plea not to break off prematurely out of self-righteousness this mutual questioning process of correction. For the truth of the gospel, whose thrust is towards historical — and that means social — embodiment, can be acknowledged only in fellowship, and only in the clash of debate.

If this is correct, then the "conciliar process" offers in fact a very concrete testing ground for learning to live in the "ecumenical household". The basic rules for relations between the members of God's household outlined above then become criteria for the conduct of the churches in the conciliar process, indeed at all levels of their life. Self-restraint and striving for truth in dialogue, sharing in solidarity with one another, and readiness to correct oneself in the course of ecumenical learning — these describe the dimensions of hope in a new vision of the ecumenical movement. The churches and the WCC are being invited to overcome their ecumenical uncertainty and to acknowledge that they are already living as members in God's larger household.

# *Postscript*

This book was written three years ago with a German audience in mind. It draws heavily on material from the discussion in Germany among people who are committed to and concerned about the ecumenical movement. The response which the book has received so far seems to indicate that it has been able to meet its intended purpose, i.e. to stimulate a critical assessment and to open up new perspectives for understanding the ecumenical calling.

It is always somewhat of a risk to translate reflections which are rooted in a particular context into a different setting. I am very much indebted to Tony Coates who has succeeded admirably in rendering my thoughts into fluent English. At the same time, I want to express my thanks to the Publications Board of the WCC for its interest in making available an English edition of this book. As the preface indicates, I have written these chapters in silent dialogue not only with my students and ecumenical companions in Germany but also with the large number of friends and former colleagues in the worldwide ecumenical movement. Therefore, I am glad that the barrier of language no longer limits that extended dialogue and common reflection which this study wants to serve.

The text has been edited and slightly abridged for this English edition, making it less academic and leaving out exclusively German references, especially in the footnotes. Nevertheless, the argument may appear very German to many English-language readers, particularly with its emphasis on historical analysis and on systematic construction. I can only hope that it will be understood, also among its new readers, as an invitation for critical, forward-looking dialogue.

The initial motivation for writing this study was the desire to gain a better understanding of the present condition of the ecumenical movement, its uncertainty and lack of vision. Is the so-called "crisis" of the ecumenical movement a sign of decline and possibly disintegration or is it a manifestation of growth and transformation? For any diagnosis of a "critical condition" it makes a basic difference which perspective is being chosen: the conservative view of preservation or the one looking forward to a new integration. This book is written out of the conviction that the ecumenical movement finds itself in the midst of such a process of transformation. It wants to encourage an explorative attitude overcoming the tendency of merely defending old positions.

In order to substantiate my rather simple thesis, which is ultimately rooted in an act of faith, I have taken up the notion of a "paradigm shift" as developed by Thomas S. Kuhn. Since this concept has gained prominence among the advocates and followers of "New Age"-thinking I want to underline that its role in my study is limited to that of an analytical tool, an heuristic device which is meant to focus attention on certain features which would otherwise remain obscure or unconnected.

Whether my attempt to reconstruct what I call the "classical ecumenical paradigm" does justice to the past, and whether I have succeeded in identifying the points where this paradigm has been challenged, will have to be judged by others involved in the ecumenical dialogue. This applies even more to the endeavour of indicating elements of an emerging new paradigm. The "experimental" character of the argument needs to be kept in mind in all its stages. It is not my intention to proclaim a "new paradigm" which should replace the old one. A new and common vision of the ecumenical movement can only emerge out of the continuing ecumenical dialogue itself. Even less am I suggesting a simple break of continuity in the process of transition from the "old" to the "new". In fact, the notion of "paradigm shift" implies that any new frame of orientation can claim validity only to the extent that it succeeds in preserving and integrating the truth contained in earlier perceptions. Therefore, it is not a matter of replacing the "Christocentric universalism" of the past, but of integrating it into a more comprehensive perspective that meets the challenges and contradictions which have arisen.

Since this book was first published, the ecumenical movement has moved on. In particular, the preliminary results of the JPIC process and the discussions at the seventh assembly of the WCC in Canberra (February 1991) throw new light on several facets of this present study. The two issues presented as "test samples" in the concluding chapter could now be discussed less tentatively and the effort of assessing the validity of the whole argument could be extended to other areas, like the question of the community of women and men, which have not been adequately treated in this study.

Having participated actively both in the JPIC world convocation at Seoul 1990 and in the recent WCC assembly at Canberra, I feel, however, strengthened in my conviction that ecumenism is caught in a process of transition. I find additional evidence for the challenges confronting the inherited frame of reference, e.g. the unresolved tension at Seoul between a global, analytical approach and the insistence on the primacy of contextual struggles, the inconclusive debate in Canberra about the danger of "syncretism" in the encounter between gospel and culture, the renewed emergence of the question where to draw the limits of diversity in the search for the unity of the church, and the issue of anthropocentrism in the approach to creation.

At the same time, the theme of the Canberra assembly, "Come, Holy Spirit — Renew the Whole Creation", has reinforced the process, begun already at the Vancouver assembly in 1983, of widening the scope of ecumenical reflection beyond the traditional Christocentric interpretation of human history. Even if the discussion at Canberra has not yet achieved the breakthrough towards a fully Trinitarian understanding of the wholeness of the *oikoumene*, it has stimulated again the search for a "vital and coherent theology".

It is my hope that the present study may be able to make a contribution to this search and thus will further the process of renewal which the Canberra assembly has placed in the centre of the programme policies for the WCC in the years to come.

May 1991                                                           *Konrad Raiser*

# Notes

*Translator's note:* Generally notes are only given referring to works available in English, or where an actual quotation, not available in English, has been translated from the German. Fuller notes referring to works available only in German appear in Dr Raiser's original German edition.

*Works frequently cited*

ER = *The Ecumenical Review*

Uppsala report = Norman Goodall ed., *The Uppsala Report 1968*, WCC, Geneva, 1968.

Louvain report = Lukas Vischer ed., *Faith and Order: Louvain 1971. Study Reports and Documents*, Faith and Order Paper No. 59, WCC, Geneva, 1971.

Nairobi report = David M. Paton ed., *Breaking Barriers: Nairobi 1975*, SPCK, London, and Wm B. Eerdmans, Grand Rapids, 1976.

Vancouver report = David Gill ed., *Gathered for Life: Official Report, Sixth Assembly, World Council of Churches*, WCC, Geneva, and Wm B. Eerdmans, Grand Rapids, 1983.

*Doc. Hist.* = Lukas Vischer ed., *A Documentary History of the Faith and Order Movement 1927-1963*, Bethany Press, St Louis, 1963.

Biblical quotations are mostly from *The Revised English Bible*, © Oxford University Press and Cambridge University Press 1989.

## 1. Uncertainty in the Ecumenical Movement

[1] Ernst Lange, *And Yet It Moves. Dream and Reality of the Ecumenical Movement*, WCC, Geneva; CJL, Belfast; and Wm B. Eerdmans, Grand Rapids, 1979, pp.107ff. (the date 1972 refers to the German edition).

[2] Cf. Constitution of the WCC, III (1), in Vancouver Report, p.324.

[3] Constantin G. Patelos ed., *The Orthodox Church in the Ecumenical Movement: Documents and Statements 1902-1975*, WCC, Geneva, 1978, p.97.

[4] Joseph Ratzinger, *Church, Ecumenism and Politics*, St Paul Publications, Slough, and Crossroad, New York, 1988, p.138.

[5] Cf. O.H. Pesch in "Ökumenismus der Bekehrung — in der Zerreissprobe der Logik", in H. Fries & O.H. Pesch, *Streiten für die eine Kirche*, Munich, 1987, pp.135ff.

[6] *Ibid.*, p.149.

[7] Cf. the statement of the WCC central committee, Rolle, Switzerland, 1951, on "The Calling of the Church to Mission and to Unity", in *Doc. Hist.*, pp.177ff.

[8] Dogmatic Constitution on the Church, *Lumen Gentium*, para. 1, in Austin Flannery ed., *Vatican Council II*, Dominican Publications, Dublin, 1988, p.350.

[9] Uppsala report, p.17.

[10] Encyclical letter of Pope Paul VI, *Populorum Progressio*, Catholic Truth Society, London, 1967, p.35.

[11] Cf. Konrad Raiser, "Beyond Collaboration: Perspectives on the Work of the Joint Working Group between the Roman Catholic Church and the WCC, 1972-1982", in *ER*, Vol. 35, No. 2, April 1983, pp.179ff.

[12] "Committed to Fellowship: A Letter to the Churches", adopted by the central committee of the WCC, Utrecht, 1972, in *ER*, Vol. 24, No. 4, 1972, pp.474-78.

[13] Vancouver report, p.49.

[14] Cf. particularly Thomas. F. Best ed., *Beyond Unity-in-Tension*, WCC, Geneva, 1988, esp. the introductory chapter by the editor and note 3 (p.28), which lists the principal texts to date. Cf. also Gennadios Limouris ed., *Church, Kingdom, World. The Church as Mystery and Prophetic Sign*, WCC, Geneva, 1986.

[15] Cf. the draft study "Christ, the Holy Spirit and the Ministry", in *Commission on Faith and Order, Minutes of the Meeting in 1964 in Aarhus, Denmark*, WCC, Geneva, 1965, pp.47ff.; cf. also the study "The Ordained Ministry", in Louvain report, pp.78ff.

[16] *Baptism, Eucharist and Ministry*, WCC, Geneva, 1982.

[17] Cf. report of Section V, "Worship", in Uppsala report, pp.74ff.; and the study "Worship today", in Louvain report, pp.102ff.

[18] Cf. report of the moderator of the central committee, M.M. Thomas, in Nairobi report, pp.226ff.

[19] Cf. "An Ecumenical Programme to Combat Racism", in *ER*, Vol. 21, No. 4, 1969, pp.348-53, esp. p.353.

[20] Cf. esp. report of Issue Group 6 "Struggling for Justice and Human Dignity", in Vancouver report, pp.83-91, esp. paras 7 and 26.

[21] Decree on Ecumenism, para. 8, in Flannery, *op. cit.*, p.460.

[22] On dialogue as a method, cf. the comprehensive study by K. Pathil, *Models in Ecumenical Dialogue. A Study of the Methodological Development in the Commission on Faith and Order of the WCC*, Bangalore, India, 1981.

[23] Cf. E. Schlink, *Ökumenische Dogmatik*, Göttingen, 1983, p.696.

[24] "On the Ecumenical Dialogue. A Working Paper prepared by the Joint Working Group between the WCC and the Roman Catholic Church", in *ER*, Vol. 19, No. 4, 1967, pp.469-73.

[25] Cf. *Ökumenische Rundschau*, 1988, No. 2, pp.205ff: this quotation on p.218.

[26] For the text of the Leuenberg agreement, cf. *ER*, Vol. 25, No. 3, 1973, pp.355-59.

[27] This is the interpretation of O.H. Pesch "Die Lehrverurteilungen des 16. Jahrhunderts und die ökumenische Situation der Gegenwart", in H. Fries & O.H. Pesch, *op. cit.*, pp.85ff, esp. pp.130ff.; cf. also Karl Lehmann & Wolfhart Pannenberg eds, *The Condemnations of the Reformation Era: Do They Still Divide?*, Fortress Press, Minneapolis, 1990.

[28] Cf. Konrad Raiser, "Growing into the Ecumenical Covenant: Reflections on the Occasion of the 60th Anniversary of the 1925 Stockholm Conference", in W. Schmidt ed., *Catalyzing Hope for Justice: A Tribute to C.I. Itty*, WCC, Geneva, 1987, pp.50ff.

[29] Cf. the material in K. Srisang ed., *Perspectives on Political Ethics: An Ecumenical Enquiry*, WCC, Geneva, including my contribution "Continuing an Old Discussion in a New Context".

[30] Cf. *The Kairos Document*, CIIR/BCC, London, 1985, pp.9ff.

[31] Cf. Paulo Freire, *Pedagogy of the Oppressed*, Sheed & Ward, London, and Penguin Books, London, 1972; and Ernst Lange, *Sprachschule für die Freiheit. Bildung als Problem und Funktion der Kirche*, Munich, Gelnhausen, 1980.

[32] Cf. *Ökumenisches Lernen. Grundlagen und Impulse*, Kirchenamt der EKD, Gütersloh, 1985, esp. p.17.

[33] Ernst Lange, "The Malaise in the Ecumenical Movement. Notes on the Present Situation", in *ER*, Vol. 23, No. 1, 1971, pp.1-8. This quotation p.8.

[34] Cf. Ernst Lange, *Kirche für die Welt*, Munich, Gelnhausen, 1981, p.301.

[35] The Toronto statement is reproduced in *Doc. Hist.*, pp.167ff.; and in W.A. Visser 't Hooft, *The Genesis and Formation of the World Council of Churches*, WCC, Geneva, 1982, pp.112ff.

[36] Cf. Werner Simpfendörfer, "Die Utopie entlässt ihre Kinder. Was wird aus der ökumenischen Bewegung?", in *Evang. Kommentare*, 12/1987, p.715.

## 2. The Classical Self-understanding of the Ecumenical Movement

[1] Words from a paper by E. Jüngel at a symposium in Tübingen.

[2] Thomas S. Kuhn, *The Structure of Scientific Revolutions*, University of Chicago Press, Chicago, 2nd ed., 1970, p.175.

[3] Cf. esp. W.A. Visser 't Hooft, *No Other Name: The Choice between Syncretism and Christian Universalism*, SCM, London, 1963, pp.103ff.

[4] *Ibid.*, pp.103-113.

[5] *Ibid.*, p.107.

[6] *Ibid.*, p.108.

[7] *Ibid.*, p.110.

[8] *Ibid.*, p.113.

[9] Cf. the statement "The Missionary Calling of the Church", in *International Review of Missions*, Vol. 41, No. 164, 1952, "Quarterly Notes".

[10] *Doc. Hist.*, p.178.

[11] W.A. Visser 't Hooft ed., *The Evanston Report: The Second Assembly of the World Council of Churches 1954*, SCM, London, 1955.

[12] Cf. "The Message of the First Assembly of the WCC", Amsterdam, 1948, in *Doc. Hist.*, pp.75-84, esp. pp.76-77.

[13] "A Word to the Churches", in O.S. Tomkins ed., *The Third World Conference on Faith and Order, Lund, 1952*, SCM, London, 1953, p.15.

[14] Report of the Theological Commission on Christ and the Church, Faith and Order Paper No. 38, WCC, Geneva, 1963.

[15] W.A. Visser 't Hooft, *The Kingship of Christ: An Interpretation of Recent European Theology*, SCM, London, 1948.

[16] G.K.A. Bell, *The Kingship of Christ: The Story of the World Council of Churches*, Penguin, Harmondsworth, 1954, p.12.

[17] Cf. "The Lordship of Christ over the World and the Church", study document, WCC Division of Studies, Geneva, 1959.

[18] *Ibid.*, p.3.

[19] *Ibid.*, pp.10-11.

[20] W.A. Visser 't Hooft, "The Calling of the World Council of Churches", report of the general secretary to the third assembly of the WCC at New Delhi, in *ER*, Vol. 14, No. 2, 1962, p.224.

[21] Decree on Ecumenism, para. 11, in Flannery, *op. cit.*, p.462.

[22] W.A. Visser 't Hooft, "Die Periode der Universalität", address in the Week of Prayer for Christian Unity in Brussels 1966, in *Ökumenischer Aufbruch, Hauptschriften*, Vol. 2, Stuttgart, Berlin, p.267.

[23] Konrad Raiser, "Confessing the Lord Jesus Christ as God and Saviour", in *ER*, Vol. 37, No. 2, 1985, pp.182ff. The comments which follow are taken, in part word for word, from that article; cf. also the other articles in that issue devoted to the WCC basis.

[24] Cited in Visser 't Hooft, *The Genesis and Formation of the WCC, op. cit.*, p.50.

[25] Cf. Geiko Müller-Fahrenholz, *Heilsgeschichte zwischen Ideologie und Prophetie*, Freiburg, Basle, Vienna, 1974, p.41.

[26] *Ibid.*, pp.42ff.

[27] Cf. Konrad Raiser, "Inkarnation und Kreuz", in *Als Boten des gekreuzigten Herrn*, Berlin, 1982, pp.47ff.

[28] Cf. note 14 above.

[29] Cf. W.A. Visser 't Hooft, *The Kingship of Christ, op. cit.*, ch. V, pp.80ff.

[30] W.A. Visser 't Hooft, opening speech at the fourth assembly of the Conference of European Churches (Nyborg IV), unpublished manuscript in archives of the Conference of European Churches. The German translation of this speech (which was given in English) appears in *Zusammen Leben als Kontinente und Generationen. Nyborg IV/64*, Gotthelf-Verlag, Zürich, Frankfurt a.M., pp.83ff.

[31] Cf. Geiko Müller-Fahrenholz, *op. cit.*, pp.20ff.

[32] *Ibid.*, part II, pp.67-192.

[33] *Ibid.*, p.33.

[34] *Ibid.*, p.38.

[35] Cf. W.A. Visser 't Hooft ed., *The New Delhi Report: The Third Assembly of the World Council of Churches, 1961*, SCM, London, 1962, p.15.

[36] "God in Nature and History", in *New Directions in Faith and Order, Bristol, 1967*, WCC, Geneva, 1968.

[37] *Ibid.*, p.29.

[38] A.Th. van Leeuwen, *Christianity in World History: The Meeting of the Faiths of East and West*, Edinburgh House, London, 1964.

[39] *The Church for Others and the Church for the World. A Quest for Structures for Missionary Congregations*, WCC, Geneva, 1967.

[40] W.A. Visser 't Hooft, *No Other Name, op. cit.*

[41] *Ibid.*, p.74.

[42] *Ibid.*, p.95.

[43] *Ibid.*, p.101.

[44] *Ibid.*, p.102.

[45] *Ibid.*, pp.102-103.

[46] Cf. H. Berkhof, "The Finality of Jesus Christ", in Uppsala report, *op. cit.*, pp.304ff.

[47] *Ibid.*, pp.307-308.

[48] This critical questioning is explicitly developed in Kristen E. Skydsgaard, "The Hidden-ness of God and the Unity of the Church", in Reinhard Groscurth ed., *What Unity Implies. Six Essays after Uppsala*, WCC, Geneva, 1969, pp.53ff; cf. also para. 21 in Berkhof's address in Uppsala report, p.309.

## 3. The New Challenges Facing the Ecumenical Movement

[1] Cf. Nairobi report, pp.70ff; for an interpretation of the debate cf. S.J. Samartha, *Courage for Dialogue. Ecumenical Issues in Inter-religious Relationships*, WCC, Geneva, and Maryknoll Books, New York, 1981, pp.49ff.

[2] *Guidelines on Dialogue with People of Living Faiths and Ideologies*, WCC, Geneva, 1979; on the Vancouver debate, cf. Vancouver report, pp.31ff.

[3] Cf. C.F. Hallenkreutz, *New Approaches to Men of Other Faiths*, WCC, Geneva, 1969; and *idem*, *Dialogue and Community*, WCC, Geneva, 1977, and, more recently, the edition of the *International Review of Mission* with the theme "Tambaram Revisited", Vol. 78, No. 307, July 1988.

[4] Cf. Hendrik Kraemer, *The Christian Message in a non-Christian World*, Edinburgh House Press, London, 1938; for Visser 't Hooft's position cf. ch. II; for Lesslie Newbigin's position cf. *The Open Secret*, SPCK, London, and Wm. B. Eerdmans, Grand Rapids, 1978.

[5] On the "inclusive" position, cf. C.F. Hallenkreutz, *op. cit.*, chs 3 and 4, pp.35ff; A. Race, *Christians and Religious Pluralism*, New York, 1982, pp.38ff; M.M. Thomas, *Risking Christ for Christ's Sake*, WCC, Geneva, 1987, pp.19ff.

[6] Cf. S.J. Samartha, *op. cit.*, p.88; John Hick, *God Has Many Names*, Macmillan, London, 1980; A. Race, *ibid.*, esp. pp.106ff; and Wesley Ariarajah, *The Bible and People of Other Faiths*, WCC, Geneva, 1985, pp.58ff.

[7] Cf. S.J. Samartha, *op. cit.*, p.96; W. Ariarajah, *op. cit.*, pp.64ff.

[8] Cf. Metropolitan Georges Khodre, "Christianity in a Pluralistic World — the Economy of the Holy Spirit", in *ER*, Vol. 23, No. 2, 1971, pp.118-28; and S. Samartha, *op. cit.*, pp.63ff.

[9] The most important documentation from this study has been brought together in Geiko Müller-Fahrenholz ed., *Unity in Today's World: The Faith and Order Studies on "Unity of the Church — Unity of Humankind"*, WCC, Geneva, 1978.

[10] Cf. the comments in the report presented to the Faith and Order Commission at Bristol, 1967, in *New Directions in Faith and Order, op. cit.*, pp.19ff.

[11] Cf. Müller-Fahrenholz, *op. cit.*, p.91.

[12] Cf. "An Ecumenical Programme to Combat Racism", in *ER*, Vol. 21, No. 4, 1969, pp.348-353.

[13] "Threats to Survival" appears in *Study Encounter*, Vol. 10, No. 4, 1974, SE/67, pp.1ff.; "The Economic Threat to Peace" in *ER*, Vol. 27, No. 1, 1975, pp.67ff.; and the report of the Bucharest conference, "Science and Technology for Human Development: The

Ambiguous Future and the Christian Hope", in *Anticipation*, No. 19, 1974. For the reaction of the central committee, cf. Minutes of the Meeting in Berlin (West), August 1974.

[14] The report on "The Search for a Just, Participatory and Sustainable Society" is reproduced in K. Srisang ed., *Perspectives on Political Ethics: An Ecumenical Enquiry*, WCC, Geneva, 1983, appendix; for the debate, cf. Minutes of the Meeting of the central committee in Kingston, Jamaica, January 1979, pp.16ff.

[15] Cf. M. Arruda ed., *Ecumenism and a New World Order: The Failure of the 1970s and the Challenges of the 1980s*, Vol. 1 of the series "An Ecumenical Approach to Economics", WCC, Geneva, 1980.

[16] Cf. *Churches and the Transnational Corporations: An Ecumenical Programme*, WCC, Geneva, 1983, p.14.

[17] Thomas Wieser ed., *Whither Ecumenism? A Dialogue in the Transit Lounge of the Ecumenical Movement*, WCC, Geneva, 1986, pp.29-30.

[18] This formula was used by the Evangelical Church in the GDR from 1983 to describe the system of deterrence.

[19] Cf. Th. Wieser, *op. cit.*, "Reflections" on pp.35ff, and the Bible studies by Philip Potter on Gen. 11 and Rev. 21 on pp.9ff.

[20] Cf. Philip Potter's closing address in Nairobi report, p.208.

[21] Cf. the contribution to the debate by C.T. Kurien, in R. Shinn ed., *Faith and Science in an Unjust World*, WCC, Geneva, 1980, pp.220ff.; cf. also "Integrity of Creation: An Ecumenical Discussion", mimeographed report of a WCC consultation at Granvollen, Norway, 1988, which raised the debate to a new level.

[22] Cf. Claus Westermann, *Blessing in the Bible and the Life of the Church*, Fortress Press, Minneapolis, 1978; and Gerhard von Rad, *Wisdom in Israel*, SCM, London, 1972.

[23] Jürgen Moltmann, *God in Creation: An Ecological Doctrine of Creation*, SCM, London, 1985, p.278.

[24] Leonardo Boff, *Ecclesiogenesis: The Base Communities Reinvent the Church*, Collins, London, and Orbis Books, New York, 1986.

[25] Cf. the "Zagorsk document 1973" in Geiko Müller-Fahrenholz, *Unity in Today's World, op. cit.*, pp.78ff, esp. p.84.

[26] *Ibid.*, p.85.

[27] Cf. Christian Duquoc, *Provisional Churches: An Essay in Ecumenical Ecclesiology*, SCM, London, 1986, pp.107ff.

[28] Of particular importance here is John D. Zizioulas, *Being as Communion*, DLT, London, 1985.

## 4. The "Oikoumene": the One Household of Life

[1] Vancouver report, p.251.

[2] *Ibid.*, p.249.

[3] *Ibid.*, p.249.

[4] *Ibid.*, p.254.

[5] José Míguez Bonino, "The Concern for a Vital and Coherent Theology", in *ER*, Vol. 41, No. 2, 1989, pp.160ff.: this quotation p.164.

[6] *Ibid.*, pp.166-67.

[7] Werner Simpfendörfer, "Quo Vadis — Oikoumene?", in Th. Wieser, *op. cit.*, p.x.

[8] Philip Potter, *Life in All Its Fullness*, Wm B. Eerdmans, Grand Rapids, and WCC, Geneva, 1981, p.162.

⁹ *Guidelines on Dialogue, op. cit.*, pp.10-11.

¹⁰ Cf. Nairobi report, pp.245ff.; Vancouver report, pp.193ff.; *ER*, Vol. 29, No. 4, 1977, pp.354ff.; *ER*, Vol. 31, No. 2, 1979, pp.133ff; *ER*, Vol. 32, No. 4, 1980, pp.377ff.; and *ER*, Vol. 33, No. 4, 1981, pp.330ff.

¹¹ Vancouver report, pp.193ff.

¹² *Ibid.*, p.197.

¹³ Cf. W.A. Visser 't Hooft, *The Meaning of Ecumenical*, SCM, London, 1953.

¹⁴ Cf. "The Calling of the Church to Mission and to Unity", received by the central committee, Rolle, 1951, in *Doc. Hist.*, pp.177-78.

¹⁵ Decree on Ecumenism, para I.4, in Flannery, *op. cit.*, pp.456-59.

¹⁶ Philip Potter, report of the general secretary, in *ER*, Vol. 25, No. 4, 1973, pp.416-17.

¹⁷ Cf. Klaus Wengst, *Pax Romana and the Peace of Jesus Christ*, SCM, London, 1987.

¹⁸ Ernst Lange, "The Malaise in the Ecumenical Movement. Notes on the Present Situation", in *ER*, Vol. 23, No. 1, 1971, pp.1-8: this quotation p.8.

¹⁹ Jürgen Moltmann, *God in Creation: An Ecological Doctrine of Creation*, SCM, London, 1985. After completing this manuscript, I discovered L.M. Russell, *Household of Freedom: Authority in Feminist Theology*, Philadelphia, 1986. I gratefully acknowledge the confirmation of my own thinking provided by this very similar approach.

²⁰ Moltmann, *ibid.*, p.142.

²¹ *Ibid.*, p.144.

²² Cf. Claus Westermann, *Genesis: A Commentary*, SPCK, London, and Augsburg Publishing House, 1984-87, Vol. 1, 1984.

²³ Cf. article on "oikos" by Otto Michel, in Gerhard Kittel ed., *Theological Dictionary of the New Testament*, Vol. V, Wm B. Eerdmans, Grand Rapids, 1967, pp.119ff.; and article on "skene" by Wilhelm Michaelis, in Gerhard Friedrich ed., *ibid.*, Vol. VII, 1971, pp.368ff.

²⁴ Cf. Matt. 24:43ff.; 25:14ff.; Luke 12:39ff.; 16:11ff.

²⁵ In Mark 3:24ff. and Matt. 12:25 "kingdom" and "house(hold)" are in parallel. For the relation between "house(hold)" and "father" cf. John 8:35; 14:2.

²⁶ Cf. esp. M. Douglas Meeks, "Economic Justice and Common Mission", in *EKU/UCC Newsletter*, VI/1, 1985, pp.9-26.

²⁷ Cf. report of section I, "The Holy Spirit and the Catholicity of the Church", in Uppsala report, pp.7ff.; and Reinhard Groscurth, *What Unity Implies*, WCC, Geneva, 1969; on the filioque controversy, cf. Lukas Vischer ed., *Spirit of God, Spirit of Christ*, SPCK, London, and WCC, Geneva, 1981.

²⁸ Cf. Jürgen Moltmann, *The Trinity and the Kingdom of God*, SCM, London, 1981; J. Zizioulas, *Being as Communion*, DLT, London, 1985; Leonardo Boff, *Trinity and Society*, Burns & Oates, Tunbridge Wells, 1988.

²⁹ Cf. esp. the first two chapters in J. Zizioulas, *ibid.*, pp.37-122.

³⁰ Moltmann, *Trinity, op. cit.*, p.69.

³¹ *Ibid.*, p.69.

³² *Ibid.*, p.70.

³³ Cf. Walter Kasper, "Die Kirche als Sakrament des Geistes", in W. Kasper & G. Sauter, *Kirche — Ort des Geistes*, Freiburg, 1976, p.31.

³⁴ Boff, *op. cit.*, pp.139-40.

³⁵ Moltmann, *Trinity, op. cit.*, pp.198-99.

³⁶ Vancouver report, p.44-45.

³⁷ The term "eucharistic vision" was introduced by P. Lonning into the work of issue group 2 at Vancouver, "Taking Steps Towards Unity".

[38] Cf. previous chapter for relevant texts of the Commission on Faith and Order. On Roman Catholic developments in communion-ecclesiology, cf. J.-M.R. Tillard, *Eglise d'églises. L'écclesiologie de communion*, Editions du Cerf, Paris, 1987 (English translation in preparation); also Walter Kasper, *Theology and Church*, SCM, London, 1989. This ecclesiology was officially received by the Extraordinary Synod of Bishops in 1985.

[39] The founder of "eucharistic ecclesiology" is considered to be the Russian theologian Nicolas Afanassieff. Cf. "The Church which Presides in Love", in N. Afanassieff et al., *The Primacy of Peter in the Orthodox Church*, Faith Press, Leighton Buzzard, 1963, pp.57ff.

[40] The Didache, as quoted on p.5 of Vancouver report.

[41] For the essential significance of the office of bishop in eucharistic ecclesiology for maintaining fellowship between local churches, which cannot be examined here, cf. Zizioulas, *op. cit.*, chapters 4, 6 & 7.

[42] Cf. H. Dombois, *Das Recht der Gnade. Ökumenisches Kirchenrecht II*, Bielefeld, 1974, pp.35ff.

[43] Cf. Wolfgang Huber, *Kirche*, Munich, 1988; Ulrich Duchrow, *Conflict over the Ecumenical Movement. Confessing Christ Today in the Universal Church*, WCC, Geneva, 1981, pp.350ff.; and idem, *Global Economy: A Confessional Issue for the Churches?*, WCC, Geneva, 1987, pp.59ff.

[44] Cf. article on "paroikos" by K.L. and M.A. Schmidt, in Gerhard Kittel ed., *Theological Dictionary of the New Testament*, Vol. V, Wm B. Eerdmans, Grand Rapids, 1967, pp.841ff.

[45] Cf. Ernst Lange, *And Yet It Moves, op. cit.*, p.141.

[46] Cf. Gerhard Lohfink, *Jesus and Community: The Social Dimension of Christian Faith*, SPCK, London, 1985, p.146.

[47] Christian Duquoc, *Provisional Churches*, SCM, London, 1986, p.108.

[48] Quoted by John Deschner in Louvain report, p.190.

[49] Cf. John D. Zizioulas, "The Development of Conciliar Structures to the Time of the First Ecumenical Council", in *Councils and the Ecumenical Movement*, WCC, Geneva, 1968, pp.34ff.

[50] Cf. the statement by the Commission on Faith and Order "Conciliarity and the Future of the Ecumenical Movement", in Louvain report, pp.225ff.: this quotation p.226.

[51] Cf. J. Brosseder, "Gemeinschaft zuerst leben, dann darüber reden!", in *Ökumene am Ort*, No. 9/1984, pp.5ff.

[52] Cf. "Theologie der ökumene — ökumenische Theoriebildung", in *Ökumenische Rundschau* 2/1988, p.216.

[53] Cf. M. Hengel, *Property and Riches in the Early Church*, Fortress, Phildelphia, 1974, also in M. Hengel, *Earliest Christianity*, SCM Press, London, 1986; and Julio de Santa Ana, *Good News to the Poor*, WCC, Geneva, 1977.

[54] Cf. Huibert van Beek ed., *Sharing Life*, official report of the WCC world consultation on "Koinonia: Sharing Life in a World Community", WCC, Geneva, 1989, pp.36ff.

[55] Cf. J. Rossel, *Teilen in ökumenischer Gemeinschaft, Texte zum Kirchlichen Entwicklungsdienst*, 32, Frankfurt, 1973, p.13.

[56] Towards an Ecumenical Commitment for Resource Sharing, Office for resource sharing, WCC, Geneva, 1984, p.10.

[57] Cf. Philip Potter's report to the Vancouver assembly in Vancouver report, pp.193ff.; also in *ER*, Vol. 35, No. 4, 1983, pp.350ff.

[58] Cf. F. Mussner, "Das Wesen des Christentums ist synesthien", in H. Rossmann & J. Ratzinger eds, *Mysterium der Gnade*, Regensburg, 1975, pp.92ff.

[59] *Ibid.*, p.100.

[60] J. Brosseder, *op. cit.*, pp.3ff.

[61] Cf. the meditation on Rublev's icon entitled *The Triune God: The Supreme Source of Life* (video), WCC, Geneva; also Vancouver report, p.26.

## 5. Two Areas of Paradigm Shift

[1] Cf. W.A. Visser 't Hooft, "The Meaning of Membership in the WCC", in Minutes of the 17th Meeting of WCC central committee, 1963, pp.134-38: this quotation p.138.

[2] Cf. Nairobi report, appendix 6, pp.271ff.: this quotation pp.272-73.

[3] Vancouver report, p.209.

[4] The proposal appears in the report of the consultation of representatives of the Orthodox WCC member churches in Sofia, May 1981, in Todor Sabev ed., *The Sofia Consultation: Orthodox Involvement in the World Council of Churches*, WCC, Geneva, 1982, p.23. The decision on the proposal was taken by the WCC executive committee at its meeting in Geneva in spring 1983.

[5] Cf. Thomas Stransky, "A Basis Beyond the Basis", in *ER*, Vol. 37, No. 2, 1985, pp.213ff.

[6] *Ibid.*, p.222.

[7] Cf. report of the assembly's Programme Guidelines Committee in Vancouver report, p.255.

[8] Cf. the recommendations of issue group 6 at Vancouver, "Struggling for Justice and Human Dignity", para. 25, which led to the assembly decision, in *ibid.*, p.89. NB: the verbs "confess", "resist", "repudiate", "make... commitment", "reject".